5/11

CRIMINAL
INVESTIGATIONS

SERIAL KILLERS

CRIMINAL INVESTIGATIONS

CRIMINAL
INVESTIGATIONS

SERIAL KILLERS

MICHAEL NEWTON

CONSULTING EDITOR: **JOHN L. FRENCH,**
CRIME SCENE SUPERVISOR,
BALTIMORE POLICE CRIME LABORATORY

CHELSEA HOUSE
PUBLISHERS
An imprint of Infobase Publishing

CRIMINAL INVESTIGATIONS: Serial Killers

Chelsea House
An imprint of Infobase Publishing
132 West 31st Street
New York NY 10001

Library of Congress Cataloging-in-Publication Data
Newton, Michael, 1951–
Serial killers / Michael Newton, John L. French.
p. cm. — (Criminal investigations)
Includes bibliographical references and index.
ISBN-13: 978-0-7910-9411-2 (alk. paper)
ISBN-10: 0-7910-9411-1 (alk. paper)
1. Serial murderers—United States—Juvenile literature. 2. Serial
murders—United State—Juvenile literature. 3. Criminal investigation—
United State—Juvenile literature. 4. Serial murderers—Juvenile literature.
5. Serial murders—Juvenile literature. I. French, John L. II. Title.
  HV6529.N48 2008   364.152′3—dc22
            2007049943

Chelsea House books are available at special discounts when purchased
in bulk quantities for businesses, associations, institutions,
or sales promotions. Please call our Special Sales Department
in New York at (212) 967-8800 or (800) 322-8755.

You can find Chelsea House on the World Wide Web at
http://www.chelseahouse.com

Text design by Erika K. Arroyo
Cover design by Ben Peterson

Cover: This letter from the Zodiac killer was mailed to the *San Francisco
Chronicle* on June 26, 1970. The cypher at the bottom remains unsolved.

Printed in the United States of America

Bang EJB 10 9 8 7 6 5 4 3 2

This book is printed on acid-free paper.

All links and Web addresses were checked and verified to be
correct at the time of publication. Because of the dynamic nature
of the Web, some addresses and links may have changed
since publication and may no longer be valid.

Contents

Foreword

In 2000 there were 15,000 murders in the United States. During that same year about a half million people were assaulted, 1.1 million cars were stolen, 400,000 robberies took place, and more than 2 million homes and businesses were broken into. All told, in the last year of the twentieth century, there were more than 11 million crimes committed in this country.*

In 2000 the population of the United States was approximately 280 million people. If each of the above crimes happened to a separate person, only 4 percent of the country would have been directly affected. Yet everyone is in some way affected by crime. Taxes pay patrolmen, detectives, and scientists to investigate it, lawyers and judges to prosecute it, and correctional officers to watch over those convicted of committing it. Crimes against businesses cause prices to rise as their owners pass on the cost of theft and security measures installed to prevent future losses. Tourism in cities, and the money it brings in, may rise and fall in part due to stories about crime in their streets. And every time someone is shot, stabbed, beaten, or assaulted, or when someone is jailed for having committed such a crime, not only they suffer but so may their friends, family, and loved ones. Crime affects everyone.

It is the job of the police to investigate crime with the purpose of putting the bad guys in jail and keeping them there, hoping thereby to punish past crimes and discourage new ones. To accomplish this a police officer has to be many things: dedicated, brave, smart, honest, and imaginative. Luck helps, but it's not required. And there's one more virtue that should be associated with law enforcement. A good police officer is patient.

Patience is a virtue in crime fighting because police officers and detectives know something that most criminals don't. It's not a secret, but most lawbreakers don't learn it until it is too late. Criminals who make money robbing people, breaking into houses, or stealing cars; who live by dealing drugs or committing murder; who spend their days on the wrong side of the law, or commit any other crimes, must remember this: a criminal has to get away with every crime he or she commits. However, to get criminals off the street and put them behind bars, the police only have to catch a criminal once.

The methods by which police catch criminals are varied. Some are as old as recorded history and others are so new that they have yet to be tested in court. One of the first stories in the Bible is of murder, when Cain killed his brother Abel (Genesis 4:1–16). With few suspects to consider and an omniscient detective, this was an easy crime to solve. However, much later in that same work, a young man named Daniel steps in when a woman is accused of an immoral act by two elders (Daniel 13:1–63). By using the standard police practice of separating the witnesses before questioning them, he is able to arrive at the truth of the matter.

From the time of the Bible to almost present day, police investigations did not progress much further than questioning witnesses and searching the crime scene for obvious clues as to a criminal's identity. It was not until the late 1800s that science began to be employed. In 1879 the French began to use physical measurements and later photography to identify repeat offenders. In the same year a Scottish missionary in Japan used a handprint found on a wall to exonerate a man accused of theft. In 1892 a bloody fingerprint led Argentine police to charge and convict a mother of killing her children, and by 1905 Scotland Yard had convicted several criminals thanks to this new science.

Progress continued. By the 1920s scientists were using blood analysis to determine if recovered stains were from the victim or suspect, and the new field of firearms examination helped link bullets to the guns that fired them.

Nowadays, things are even harder on criminals, when by leaving behind a speck of blood, dropping a sweat-stained hat, or even taking a sip from a can of soda, they can give the police everything they need to identify and arrest them.

In the first decade of the twenty-first century the main tools used by the police include

- questioning witnesses and suspects
- searching the crime scene for physical evidence
- employing informants and undercover agents
- investigating the whereabouts of previous offenders when a crime they've been known to commit has occurred
- using computer databases to match evidence found on one crime scene to that found on others or to previously arrested suspects
- sharing information with other law enforcement agencies via the Internet
- using modern communications to keep the public informed and enlist their aid in ongoing investigations

But just as they have many different tools with which to solve crime, so too do they have many different kinds of crime and criminals to investigate. There is murder, kidnapping, and bank robbery. There are financial crimes committed by con men who gain their victim's trust or computer experts who hack into computers. There are criminals who have formed themselves into gangs and those who are organized into national syndicates. And there are those who would kill as many people as possible, either for the thrill of taking a human life or in the horribly misguided belief that it will advance their cause.

The Criminal Investigations series looks at all of the above and more. Each book in the series takes one type of crime and gives the reader an overview of the history of the crime, the methods and motives behind it, the people who have committed it, and the means by which these people are caught and punished. In this series celebrity crimes will be discussed and exposed. Mysteries that have yet to be solved will be presented. Readers will discover the truth about murderers, serial killers, and bank robbers whose stories have become myths and legends. These books will explain how criminals can separate a person from his hard-earned cash, how they prey on the weak and helpless, what is being done to stop them, and what one can do to help prevent becoming a victim.

John L. French,
Crime Scene Supervisor,
Baltimore Police Crime Laboratory

* Federal Bureau of Investigation. "Uniform Crime Reports, Crime in the United States 2000." Available online. URL: http://www.fbi.gov/ucr/00cius.htm. Accessed January 11, 2008.

Introduction

"I'll help you catch him, Clarise."

With those words, in *The Silence of the Lambs,* fictional killer Hannibal "The Cannibal" Lecter volunteers to help a young detective catch another madman called "Buffalo Bill," who skins his victims. Lecter keeps his word, after a fashion, but escapes from prison in the process and remains at large today—at least, on film.

In 1992 *Silence* won five Academy Awards, including Best Motion Picture of the Year. Its success, and the ongoing popularity of similar films and novels, confirms America's dark fascination with the human monsters called serial killers.

That fascination is not new. Sensational publicity surrounded the crimes of French slayer Joseph Philippe in 1866 and London's "Jack the Ripper" in 1888. Even then, serial murder was a problem as old as human civilization itself. Today, experts cannot decide if such crimes are more common, or if new advances in reporting and detection simply make it seem that way.

In any case, we know that killers live and walk among us. Of those identified between 1900 and 2005, some 85 percent were found in the United States—a startling fact, since the United States has only 5 percent of the world's population. Some researchers feel that this disparity arises from superior police work and more detailed crime reporting in America, while others blame various factors of life in the United States—such as violent movies and TV programs, the breakdown of "traditional" families, or the decline of "old time" religion—for high rates of crime nationwide.

Even among hard-core criminals, however, serial killers stand out. They murder repeatedly, often for the simple enjoyment of killing, though some also rob their victims or collect life insurance by killing family members. A few notorious slayers have killed hundreds, while many more number their victims in dozens.

Film and fiction commonly portray serial killers either as mad geniuses (like Dr. Lecter) or as mindless zombie-like figures—but neither portrayal is accurate. On screen, Michael Myers (in the *Halloween* films) and Jason Voorhees (of *Friday the 13th* fame) hide behind masks and say nothing while stalking their victims, surviving countless gunshot wounds to kill and kill again. Some Hollywood killers (like Norman Bates, in *Psycho* and its sequels) are victims of "split" personality, unaware of their murderous urges until the last reel. Others, like the villains in *The January Man* (1989) and *Taking Lives* (2004), concoct elaborate conspiracies to hide their tracks.

As usual, however, most real-life serial killers cannot live up—or down—to the image portrayed on the screen.

In fact, most identified serial killers seem ordinary, even boring, to their friends and families. Some have histories of criminal activity or mental illness, but few expose themselves by roaming the streets in a hockey mask and waving an axe. Serial killers are often someone's neighbor, father, brother, sister, husband, wife, or even the boy or girl next door.

News reports of a serial killer's arrest often include comments from his or her neighbors, describing the suspect as quiet, peaceful, shy—the kind of individual, in short, who "would not hurt a fly," much less a dozen or a hundred human beings.

And time after time, the neighbors are proven wrong.

No common mold fits all serial killers. They include men and women of all races, nationalities, and religions. In terms of age, a few begin to kill when they are very young, around age eight or nine. Others wait for middle age, but most start in their later teens or early 20s. Those who can describe their reasons list a range of motives: sex, greed, race, revenge, or even angelic or demonic voices in their heads. Most hide behind a "mask of sanity," a seemingly normal appearance they present to the world. When examined by psychiatrists, they are not classified as legally insane.

And yet, they kill repeatedly, without remorse. Most target strangers, while some others prey on friends or members of their families. They kill with guns and knives, poison and power tools, with bombs and their bare hands. Selection of their victims is as personal—and as peculiar —as the reasons why they kill.

Serial Killers probes those questions, looks for answers, and examines the ongoing threat in a global perspective, with a focus on how law enforcement agencies identify, capture, and convict these murderers. Its 10 chapters examine different aspects of serial murder.

Chapter 1 pursues a profile of the "typical" serial killer, seeking to learn who murders, and why.

Chapter 2 briefly reviews the history of serial murder, from ancient Rome to modern times.

Chapter 3 presents some of America's most notorious serial killers and the means police used to stop them.

Chapter 4 probes the dark world of female predators who kill husbands, parents, and sometimes their own children.

Chapter 5 tracks "team" killers, ranging from deadly couples to murderous cults.

Chapter 6 explores frightening cases of doctors and nurses who kill for pleasure and profit.

Chapter 7 reviews some of the strangest and most grisly crimes on record, surpassing anything devised by Hollywood.

Chapter 8 reviews serial killers who remain at large, their cases still unsolved.

Chapter 9 surveys the global scene, with dramatic cases from Europe, Asia, Africa, and South America.

Chapter 10 examines the work of psychological profilers who track unknown killers, reviewing their record of success—or failure.

Each chapter also features sidebars that include biographies, case histories, and closer looks at the forensic methods used to capture human predators before they kill again.

The danger posed by serial killers is real. Understanding that threat is the first step toward resolving it. The journey starts here and now.

Murder by Numbers

The headlines are depressingly familiar:

"Seventh Body Found"

"No Clues in Latest Murder"

"Serial Killer at Large"

"Suspect's Arrest Stuns Neighbors"

In modern times no state or major city in America, no nation of the world, has been immune to such news. Police pursue serial murderers with every tool at their disposal, capturing eight out of 10, on average. And yet, no sooner is one predator arrested than often another emerges from the shadows. The chase begins anew, while law enforcement officers, psychologists, and criminologists attempt to answer basic, vital questions: Who commits serial murder? And why?

DEFINING THE THREAT

While serial killers have always been with us, their crimes had no formal name until the 1950s. Criminologist James Reinhardt coined the term *chain killers* in 1957, describing those slayers whose victims form a chain of death and tragedy. Three years later, German author Siegfried Kracauer was first to use the term *serial murderer* in print, describing killers who claim a series of victims, one after another, in separate crimes.

How many murders constitute a series? Authorities and sources disagree on that point, demanding anywhere from two to five or six sequential crimes. The Federal Bureau of Investigation (FBI) defines serial murder as "three or more separate events in three or more separate locations with an emotional cooling-off period between homicides."[1] Unfortunately, that definition makes no allowance for killers like Jeffrey Dahmer, who murder all their victims in one place, or for those who are caught after only two murders.

The National Institute of Justice (NIJ) published a broader definition in 1988, describing serial murder as "a series of two or more murders, committed as separate events, usually, but not always by one offender acting alone. The crimes may occur over a period of time ranging from hours to years."[2] Today, while even some FBI agents prefer the NIJ's version, other researchers insist on their own definitions.

WHO KILLS?

While there is no "typical" serial killer, a study of 2,300 cases reported worldwide provides some basic information about those who kill repeatedly. In the United States 88 percent of all identified serial killers are male, and 84 percent are Caucasian.

Their problems often began in childhood, where 43 percent claim physical or sexual abuse, and 74 percent claim psychological abuse by adult caretakers. Forty-seven percent dropped out of school before twelfth grade, and 69 percent abused alcohol before they reached legal drinking age.

Some researchers believe serial violence may spring from physical illness or brain damage. Statistics show that 29 percent of known serial killers suffered persistent childhood headaches, while 19 percent experienced seizures.

Whatever the cause, the early behavior of most serial killers was violent. Fifty-six percent set fires as children, while 36 percent admitted to torturing animals. Fifty-four percent confessed violent acts against other children, and 38 percent attacked adults.

There is no rule concerning when a serial predator first begins killing, but again, statistics are suggestive. Of those identified in the United States, 1 percent killed a person for the first time before they were 13 years old, 26 percent started killing in their teens, 45 percent in their 20s, and 24 percent in their 30s. Only 4 percent killed for the first time after turning 40, and first-time killers in their 50s numbered only 1 percent.[3]

WHY DO THEY KILL?

Despite the claim by some authors that all serial murders are sexual crimes, examination of those cases solved by police reveal a variety of motives.

Sex is the root cause in 69 percent of all cases, though a killer's idea of sexual activity may not be readily apparent. Some are excited by setting fires or prowling through a stranger's home. In the 1930s, Hungarian serial bomber Sylvestre Matuschka achieved satisfaction by causing train wrecks.

Greed motivates 14 percent of all serial killers, including those who murder relatives for life insurance or inheritance. Surprisingly, greed is the motive for 41 percent of female serial killers.

Religion motivates some 5 percent of known serial killers, including some who kill members of rival sects and others who secretly practice human sacrifice.

"Mercy" killings—2 percent of the total—are most common among serial-killing doctors and nurses, who sometimes kill patients in a misguided effort to relieve their suffering. Because so many people die naturally in hospitals and rest homes, medical killers may pass undetected for years.

Insanity sparks another 2 percent of all serial murders committed by delusional persons who lose touch with reality. As an example, "Sacramento Vampire" Richard Trenton Chase hallucinated about having a disease that turned his blood to powder in his veins, alleviated only when he drank blood from his victims.

Racism is the motive in 1 percent of American serial murders, involving persons who despise and target members of other races. Neo-Nazi gunman Joseph Paul Franklin stalked African Americans and interracial couples in the 1980s, killing 20 victims. The black "Beltway Snipers" shot whites around Washington, D.C., in 2001.

Revenge inspires another 1 percent of serial murders. Railroad fireman Rudy Bladel lost his job with the Rock Island Line in 1963, and afterward killed six railroad employees in two states over the next 15 years. In San Francisco William Hanson shot middle-aged men who resembled (but had no connection to) his sister's rapist.

Finally, 6 percent of known serial killers profess varied motives from one crime to the next. South Carolina's Donald "Pee Wee" Gaskins killed some victims for sadistic pleasure and others to conceal his daily criminal activities. While serving a life term for murder, he accepted an outside "contract," or payment, to kill a fellow inmate.[4]

WHICH KILLERS ARE EXCLUDED?

Researchers often disagree over which murderers should be included as serial killers. Is it enough to simply kill one victim after another, regardless of motive? Should war criminals or terrorists be counted? What about underworld "hit men"? Many historical outlaws and pirates killed dozens—or hundreds—of victims, but do they qualify as serial killers? And what of violent modern gang members?

In his book, *Serial Killers: The Insatiable Passion* (Charles Press Publications, 1995), psychology professor Dr. David Lester makes a persuasive case for including various types of repeat killers under the serial umbrella.[5] His list of examples includes

- Nazi war criminals from World War II, such as Dr. Josef Mengele, who serially murdered hundreds of persons in weird medical experiments at the Auschwitz death camp
- Mafia killers like Chicago's Sam Giancana, who began his career as a hit man at age 17, later rising to control organized crime in the Windy City
- Political terrorists like Germany's Ulrike Meinhof, who joined in numerous bombings, assassinations, and bank robberies during the 1970s
- Frontier outlaws like John Murrell, who robbed and killed dozens of victims before he was finally captured in 1834
- Street gang members such as "Monster" Kody Scott, who earned a fearsome reputation as a gunman for the Los Angeles Crips in the 1970s

While Dr. Lester accepts all such murderous criminals as bona fide serial killers, other authorities strongly disagree, imposing strict guidelines on who should or should not receive the serial label.

☿ WHAT'S IN A NAME?

Attempts to label and classify murder sometimes cause more problems than they solve. The FBI's system of ranking homicides, outlined in the *Crime Classification Manual*, offers a case in point.[6] In FBI terminology, single, double, and triple murder are self-explanatory terms, based on the number of victims killed in a single event. Beyond that point, however, things become confused.

Mass murder, in FBI terms, requires the death of four or more victims in a single event. Classic mass murder involves a killer whose victims are strangers, as when gunman George Hennard killed 22 persons and wounded 18 at a Texas restaurant in October 1991. Family mass murder involves the murder of relatives, as when John List shot his mother, his wife, and their three children at his New Jersey home in 1971.

The FBI defines another type of homicide, spree murder, as the killing of three or more victims in one event "of short or long duration," occurring at two or more locations. The classic example is Howard Unruh, who shot 15 neighbors in Camden, New Jersey, during a 20-minute period on September 6, 1949. Exactly how that situation differs from mass murder, other than the fact that Unruh walked around the block, is a question unanswered by spokesmen for the FBI.

Finally, the FBI defines serial murder as the killing of three or more victims at different times and locations. Only an undefined "cooling-off period" separates serial killing from spree murder—and there are other problems, as well. Technically, the FBI definition excludes killers such as John Wayne Gacy Jr., who commit all or most of their murders at one location, and those like Ukraine's Anatoly Onoprienko, who kill multiple victims in successive attacks.

Yet another problem with the FBI's definition is the classification of killers like Rhode Island's William Sarmento, who killed two young boys at different times in 1987, but who was arrested before claiming a third victim. Under the FBI's labeling system, Sarmento and others like him have no category at all. For that reason alone, many experts now prefer the NIJ's broader definition of serial murder, published in 1988.

HUNTING HUMANS

Serial killers are not bound by any firm rules about how they pursue their victims, but again, cases solved by police during the past 100 years reveal certain trends.

Worldwide, 63 percent of all identified serial killers are territorial, meaning that they hunt their prey within a given area. David Berkowitz, New York City's "Son of Sam," stalked women in the borough of Queens. Lester Harrison found all of his victims in or near Chicago's Grant Park.

Nomadic killers—those who travel widely in their search for victims—make up 29 percent of the total. Examples include Theodore Bundy, who confessed to 30 murders in states ranging from Washington to Florida, and Pedro Lopez, whose crimes spanned three countries in South America. Some of these killers may travel specifically to better conceal their crimes. Others may move around due to reasons unrelated to their murderous activities.

Stationary killers, a mere 8 percent of the total, strike repeatedly at the same location, usually their home or workplace (such as hospitals and rest homes). John Gacy buried 29 victims under his home in a Chicago suburb. Jerry Spraggins killed three unrelated tenants of the same Montclair, New Jersey, apartment between 1981 and 1983.

In terms of murder methods, while 62 percent of all killers in the United States use guns, that number shrinks to 22 percent among serial killers. A majority—51 percent—prefers personal contact with victims, by beating, stabbing, or strangling them. Another 17 percent switch off between hands-on attacks and firearms. A final 10 percent use other methods, such as poison, arson, bombs, or hit-and-run attacks with cars. Many serial killers "personalize" their crimes with hands-on contact or other means. According to FBI studies, habitual shooters are more likely to keep photos of their crimes.

VICTIM SELECTION

While most serial killers stalk "targets of opportunity"—persons who are easily abducted, such as hitchhikers and prostitutes—most also choose their victims based on specific personal characteristics. A survey of historic cases indicates that

- 65 percent of all serial murder victims are female;
- 89 percent of victims in the United States are Caucasian;
- 42 percent of identified killers claim only victims of the opposite sex, while 16 percent kill same-sex victims only, and 39 percent kill some of both genders; and
- 65 percent kill only victims of their own race, 10 percent kill victims of another race exclusively, and 11 percent fail to discriminate among victims.[7]

Those figures help forensic psychologists profile unknown killers, but as we shall see, even the best profiles are only educated guesswork. In the final analysis serial killers are as diverse and unique as any other criminals—and often, they prove more difficult to catch.

A History of Violence

During the 1970s and early 1980s, journalists often described serial murder as a "new kind of crime." But they were wrong. In fact, serial killers have preyed on humankind throughout recorded history. A few historical examples serve to prove the point.

ANCIENT ASSASSINS

The Roman Empire was renowned for its blood sports, including public battles staged between armed gladiators, or between wild animals and men. Such "games" were well attended at the Coliseum and other arenas, but Roman bloodshed was not limited to officially sanctioned spectacles.

The first recorded case of serial murder (so far) dates from 331 B.C., when Roman authorities convicted 170 women of poisoning "countless" male victims and blaming their deaths on the plague. Another Roman defendant, Calpurnius, was charged with poisoning multiple wives. Around the same time, the historian Cicero accused one Oppianicus of murdering his wife, their two sons, his brother, his father-in-law, and several more unnamed victims.[1]

The historian Horace (65–8 B.C.) described two professional killers, named Apollodorus and Canidia, who carried out numerous "contracts" with deadly hemlock in honey. Livia, wife of the Emperor Augustus (27 B.C.–14 A.D.), never faced trial, although historian Dio Cassius accused her of poisoning her husband and several grandchildren.[2]

The Emperor Caligula (37–41 A.D.), widely regarded as insane, poisoned gladiators, jockeys, and horses in attempts to rig the outcome of sporting events in his favor. Some accounts also describe him staging human sacrifices.[3]

Matters had not improved by 69 A.D., when the Emperor Galba condemned a female poisoner-for-hire named Locusta. Locusta's main client, the Emperor Nero (54–68 A.D.), ordered the murders of his mother, stepbrother, an aunt, the governor of Asia, a prefect of the Praetorian Guard, and various other victims.[4]

The year 69 also saw another poisoner, Vitellius, accused of killing his mother and numerous noble friends. One year later, a Roman subject named Asprenas was tried, condemned, and executed for the murders of 130 victims.[5]

BLUEBEARD

The legend of Bluebeard involves a man who killed numerous wives, but the real-life Bluebeard, who was of noble birth, was a brutal child-killer who also practiced black magic.

Gilles de Rais (1404–40) married a wealthy older woman at age 16, thus becoming the richest man in France. Nicknamed "Bluebeard" for the blue-black color of his whiskers, Gilles led 200 soldiers to help Joan of Arc defeat English invaders at Orleans (1428) and personally attended the coronation of King Charles VII before retiring from public life to his five large estates.

Unfortunately, Gilles's extravagant lifestyle soon exhausted his fortune, and he turned to magic in hopes of producing gold from base metals. When that failed, an ex-priest named Francisco Prelati convinced Gilles to try human sacrifice. His preferred victims were orphan children, whom Gilles killed and mutilated in gruesome rituals. Before his arrest in 1440, remains of 100 young victims were found at two of Gilles's five castles.

While Gilles refused to confess under torture, he later pled guilty when threatened with excommunication from the Catholic Church. On October 26, 1440, Gilles and two of his servants were executed.

Today, some historians claim that Gilles was "framed" by French nobles and bishops to seize his estates, but that defense does not explain the bodies of dismembered children found on his property.

KILLING COUSINS

Although described in many tales as brothers, recent evidence suggests that Micajah and Wiley Harpe were actually cousins. Both were natives of North Carolina, Micajah ("Big Harpe") was born in 1768, while Wiley ("Little Harpe") was born two years later. In 1795 they moved west with their wives and children, launching a reign of terror across the present-day states of Illinois, Kentucky, Tennessee, and Mississippi.

The Harpes specialized in robbing and murdering travelers, often hiding their crimes by gutting the bodies, weighting them with stones, and sinking them in rivers. When victims were in short supply, the cousins sometimes turned on their own children. After roaming widely on their own, they joined a band of pirates, operating from a hideout known as Cave-in-Rock on the Ohio River, in present-day Hardin County, Illinois.

While the Harpes escaped justice for most of their crimes, the wilderness could not hide them forever. In August 1799 a Kentucky posse caught Micajah fleeing the scene of his latest murder. The vigilantes shot Big Harpe, severed his head, and hung it from a nearby tree to warn off other outlaws.

Brother Wiley remained free until 1803, when he murdered fellow pirate Samuel Mason for the reward on Mason's head. Harpe delivered his trophy to authorities in Mississippi, but they soon identified him and hanged Little Harpe for his latest offense on February 8, 1804.

More than 150 years later, Walt Disney Studios sanitized the Harpe legend and presented the deadly cousins (portrayed by actors Frank Richards and Paul Newlan) in *Davy Crockett and the River Pirates*. That drama premiered on TV in 1955, then went on to the big screen in 1956.

THE FRENCH RIPPER

Joseph Vacher (1869–98) was the last of 15 children born to a poor farming family in southeastern France. Known from childhood for his violent temper, Vacher joined the army in 1890 and won promotion to corporal by threatening suicide. Two years later, after shooting a girlfriend and turning the gun on himself, he was confined to an asylum for the criminally insane.

Doctors declared Vacher "cured" in April 1894, and released him to roam the French countryside. Over the next three years, he killed at least 11 persons (some reports say 14; one claims 26). Most of Vacher's victims were mutilated, and some were scarred with human bite marks.

Police arrested Vacher in August 1897, after he attacked a woman near St. Martin, in Normandy. In custody, Vacher confessed to 11 murders, blaming his fits of rage on a rabid dog, which supposedly bit him around age eight. (If true, he would have died within a month of the attack.)

Jurors rejected that claim and convicted Vacher on one count of murder, for killing a young shepherd at Tournon in 1895. Higher courts rejected the "French Ripper's" appeal, and Vacher kept his date with the guillotine on December 31, 1898.

THE SOCIABLE INN

Joe Ball (1892–1938) was known as something of a "character" in Elmendorf, Texas (southeast of San Antonio). He ran the Sociable Inn, a tavern known for its pretty young waitresses and a pit filled with alligators where Ball entertained his customers each day at feeding time. Joe had some difficulty keeping waitresses—and wives—around the place, but the variety helped make his inn more popular.

Unfortunately, Joe Ball also had a darker side. One of his neighbors, Elton Crude, who complained about the gator pit's foul smell, disappeared one night in 1936, along with his whole family. A year later, relatives of missing waitress Minnie Gotthardt spoke to the Elmendorf police, but officers believed Ball's explanation that the girl had left town to take a better job. A second missing waitress, Julia Turner, had left her clothes behind, but Ball claimed that a quarrel with her roommate drove her from the inn.

Texas Rangers took an interest in the case when two more women disappeared from Elmendorf, one leaving a substantial bank account. Investigators found some of the missing women alive and well, but two of Ball's wives and 10 waitresses left no trace behind. Soon, Ball's handyman confessed to helping Joe feed several women to his alligators. Elton Crude then reappeared, claiming that he fled town with his wife and children after seeing Ball murder a girl in 1936.

A police officer loads alligators onto a pickup truck during the Sociable Inn murder investigation. Joe Ball, the inn's owner, fed several waitresses and two of his wives to the alligators before committing suicide. *Bettmann/Corbis*

When Rangers went to arrest Ball on September 24, 1938, he drew a pistol from the inn's cash register and shot himself fatally. The handyman received a two-year prison term, while Ball's well-fed alligators found a new home at San Antonio's zoo.

Four decades later, Tobe Hooper (of *Texas Chainsaw Massacre* fame) directed a horror film titled *Eaten Alive* (1977), loosely based on Ball's crimes. The lead character, "Judd" (played by Neville Brand), runs the Starlight Hotel, where guests check in but never check out—thanks to a crocodile living under the porch.

LETHAL LOVERS

Americans worried much about "juvenile delinquents" in the 1950s, concerned by the influence on teenagers of movies like James Dean's *Rebel Without a Cause* (1955). One young viewer who idolized Dean was Charles Starkweather (1940–59), a garbage collector in Lincoln, Nebraska, who loved guns and hated most people. In 1958 with 14-year-old girlfriend Caril Ann Fugate, Starkweather became the target of the Midwest's greatest manhunt since the 1930s.

Starkweather's crime spree actually began in December 1957, when he robbed and killed a Lincoln gas station attendant. Seven weeks later, on January 21, 1958, Starkweather quarreled with Fugate's parents, who disapproved of his relationship with their daughter. Enraged, he shot Fugate's mother and stepfather, and then strangled her two-year-old sister.

Starkweather and Fugate spent six nights in the murder house, then embarked on a bloody run across the country, killing seven more victims and eluding 200 National Guardsmen before they were finally captured on February 1, 1958. At trial, Starkweather accepted full blame for the crimes and received a death sentence, then changed his story and blamed Caril Ann for killing their three female victims. Fugate denied any murders, but jurors convicted her on one count, imposing a life sentence. Starkweather died in the electric chair on June 24, 1959. Fugate remained in prison until 1976.

As Starkweather drew at least some of his inspiration from movies, so his story has inspired certain Hollywood directors. In *Badlands* (1973), Martin Sheen and Sissy Spacek portrayed "Kit and Holly," young lovers entranced by violence. Twenty years later, *Murder in the Heartland* (1993) cast Tim Roth and Fairuza Balk as Starkweather and Fugate in a made-for-TV movie mixing fact and fiction.

⚲ "NIGHTMARE HOUSE"

Truth is stranger than fiction in the case of Herman Webster Mudgett (1860–96), better known as "H. H. Holmes." A New Hampshire native, brutalized by his religious-fanatic father, Mudgett had only one friend in childhood—and lost him, when the boy fell to his death from the second floor of an abandoned house. Mudgett stood behind him when he fell.

Later, as a medical student in Michigan, Mudgett hatched a life-insurance scheme, buying policies in the names of friends or fictitious persons, and then stealing corpses from the hospital dissection room to fake death scenes and collect the benefits. It was a short step from faking death to causing it.

Mudgett reached Chicago in 1886, posing as Dr. Henry Holmes, practicing fraud and pharmacy while he built a huge apartment complex, dubbed "The Castle." He hired and fired workmen in relays, so that none knew much about the building's secret passageways and peepholes, or the basement operating room.

When finished, Mudgett's castle rivaled any haunted house imagined by a Hollywood director. Gas vents were designed to flood the rooms with deadly fumes, while the fireplaces concealed flamethrowers. Mudgett could spy on the victims in any given room, then slide their bodies down special chutes to the basement, for cremation or dissection. He also robbed his victims and sold some of their skeletons to a medical supply house.

Many of those killed by Mudgett were visitors to Chicago's 1893 World's Fair. Mudgett finally confessed to 27 murders, but various authors speculate that 50 to 200 victims died in "Nightmare House" before Mudgett's arrest.

That came in November 1895, after another life-insurance scam went wrong. Mudgett insured accomplice Ben Pitezel in 1894, then killed him to collect the payoff. Next, he killed three of Pitezel's children to keep them from telling what they knew of the fraud. Police caught Mudgett before he could murder Pitezel's wife and two surviving children.

Although he confessed to more than two dozen murders, Mudgett only faced trial for killing Ben Pitezel. Jurors convicted him, and he was hanged on May 7, 1896. Some authors mistakenly call him America's first serial killer.

Monsters Among Us

Robert Piest was late for dinner on December 11, 1978. His mother worried, since it was unlike the 15-year-old boy to miss a meal, and that evening marked the celebration of her birthday. She had seen Robert that afternoon, at the pharmacy where he worked in Des Plaines, Illinois. Her son had been excited by the offer of a better job, with a construction company run by local contractor John Wayne Gacy Jr.

Finally, Mrs. Piest called police to report her son missing. Officers questioned Gacy (1942–94), who denied any contact with Piest, but a receipt for photographs proved that Gacy had visited the pharmacy where Piest worked on December 11. Police also learned that Gacy had served 18 months of a 10-year prison term in Iowa, during 1968–69, for sexually assaulting a young male employee.

Despite that sordid background, Gacy was well liked by his neighbors, often hosting block parties and performing as a clown at children's parties. He was also active in politics, once posing for photos with the wife of President Jimmy Carter.

After a week of surveillance, detectives visited Gacy's home again on December 19 and noticed a smell of rotting flesh from beneath the floorboards. They arrested Gacy two days later and began a thorough search.

Their findings made the headlines worldwide.

Twenty-seven corpses of boys and young men lay buried in Gacy's crawlspace. Two more were hidden on another piece of property he owned, and Gacy soon confessed to dumping five more bodies—including Rob Piest's—in the Des Plaines River. Advanced

The gutted shell of the home of convicted serial killer John Wayne Gacy awaits demolition. Twenty-nine bodies were found in the crawl space and on the grounds of Gacy's property. *AP*

decomposition made identification difficult in those days before DNA testing, and nine of Gacy's victims remain unknown today.

While confessing to 33 murders, Gacy claimed to be a victim of multiple personality disorder, blaming his crimes on an alter ego named "Jack Hanley." Jurors rejected his insanity plea and convicted Gacy on all charges in March 1980. He filed multiple appeals, retracting his insanity plea and claiming total innocence, but all his legal motions were denied. Gacy died by lethal injection on May 10, 1994.[1,2]

Gacy's case illustrates the problem of serial killers who pass unnoticed in society, concealing their crimes and otherwise behaving normally with friends and neighbors. Police may not suspect a predator in their midst until he—or she—makes a mistake and is thereby revealed. The following cases all note how killers were detected or eventually gave themselves away.

"SON OF SAM"

While Gacy's ongoing crimes went unrecognized for nearly a decade, New York City's "Son of Sam"—also known as the ".44-caliber Killer"—launched a very public reign of terror, shooting young couples in cars and on sidewalks, taunting police and reporters with rambling, often incoherent letters.

For 13 months, between July 1976 and July 1977, residents of Queens, New York, were terrorized by the night-prowling gunman who signed his letters "Son of Sam." During the brutal siege he shot 13 persons in seemingly random attacks, killing six. Comparison tests proved that the same .44-caliber pistol was used in each case, but police still needed a gun to match the bullets before they could make an arrest.

The killer's own letters described him as a "monster." "I love to hunt," he wrote. "Prowling the streets for fair game—tasty meat." He favored female targets, and police believed that one male victim was shot by accident, because he had long hair.

A fortunate break led detectives at last to the killer. On July 31, 1977, patrolmen wrote a parking ticket for a Ford Galaxy parked near the last murder scene. On August 10 detectives traced the car to 24-year-old David Berkowitz in Yonkers and found an automatic rifle in the backseat. Staking out the car, they soon arrested Berkowitz and seized the pistol used in the attacks.

In custody, Berkowitz first claimed that he was possessed by an ancient demon that was inhabiting a dog owned by neighbor Sam Carr. Before shooting any human victims, he had tried and failed to kill the dog. Several psychiatrists believed Berkowitz was insane, but Dr. David Abrahamson disagreed, persuading Berkowitz to drop the phony act.

In June 1978 Berkowitz pled guilty to six murders, receiving a 365-year prison term. A year later, he claimed that some of the murders had been committed by fellow members of a Satanic cult,

Police hold letters found in the "Son of Sam" killer's apartment in Yonkers, NY, and taken to the 84th Precinct in the Brooklyn borough of New York City. *Carlos Rene Perez/AP*

but he refused further interviews on that subject after July 10, 1979, when another inmate cut his throat in prison. Debate continues today on the cult allegations, while Berkowitz remains in prison.[3,4]

TRUE LIFE CSI CATCHES A KILLER

Theodore Robert Bundy (1946–89) was the "perfect" serial killer—handsome and charming in public, admired by his teachers and classmates in college. He volunteered with a rape-crisis hot line and once ran down a purse-snatcher, receiving commendations from police.

Unfortunately for his many victims, Bundy's smiling face concealed a mind obsessed with violence and death.

Between 1974 and 1978 Bundy raped and murdered an uncertain number of girls and young women across the United States, ranging from Washington to Florida. He later confessed to 30 slayings, but hinted in some interviews that his victims might exceed 100.

While awaiting trial for one murder in Colorado, Bundy escaped from jail in December 1977 and fled to Florida, where he claimed

℣ TAKING A BITE OUT OF CRIME

Forensic odontology involves the use of dentistry or dental records to identify unknown persons, living or deceased, who may be either criminals or victims (including persons killed in accidents or by some unknown means). Identification proceeds in different ways, depending on the investigator's goal. Where authorities seek to identify an unknown person, they normally compare dental charts or X-rays to the teeth of an unknown subject. By matching the shape, size, and configuration of teeth, along with any distinctive injuries or dental work, identity may be established with a certainty equivalent to that of fingerprints or DNA testing.

A rather different method is used to identify criminal suspects. In this application, molds and photos of a suspect's teeth are compared to bite marks found at crime scenes. The bites may be found in human flesh (resulting from a fight or sexual assault), or in some other object (as where a burglar raids a victim's refrigerator and bites into a piece of cheese). In one U.S. rape case, later fictionalized on *CSI: New York,* a rape victim bit the rubber window molding in her attacker's car, thus supporting her tale of abduction and sending the rapist to prison.

Ted Bundy's case is among the most famous on record involving forensic odontology. Bundy's distinctive bite marks, found on the body of a Florida murder victim, resulted in his conviction and ultimate execution.

several more victims. In one Florida case, where he killed two girls in a college sorority house, forensic dentistry sealed Bundy's fate.

Police found bite marks on one victim's body, which they later matched to Bundy's teeth. Bundy at first refused to let investigators photograph or make molds of his teeth, but search warrants compelled him to submit. At trial, the proof was irrefutable. Bundy, and he alone, had bitten the Florida victim. Jurors convicted him of murder, and he died in Florida's electric chair on January 24, 1989.

Before his execution, Bundy—like fiction's Dr. Hannibal Lecter—volunteered to help Washington detectives in their search for the elusive Green River Killer. Those interviews revealed much about Bundy's own strange psychology, but they brought authorities no closer to the killer still at large. Today, most experts think that Bundy's "help"—like his offers to lecture on the dangers of pornography—was simply a ploy to delay his own death. In the end, those efforts failed.[5,6]

Ironically, Bundy was memorialized in a scene from *The Silence of the Lambs*, where the killer known as "Buffalo Bill" dons a cast to pretend that his arm is broken. Bundy sometimes used that trick to gain sympathy from prospective victims and lure them within striking distance.

THE "NIGHT STALKER"

Seven years after Berkowitz filed his guilty plea in New York, an equally frightening serial killer rampaged through Los Angeles. Unlike Berkowitz, however, this one preyed on victims in their homes, with a series of late-night invasions that left 14 victims dead and eight more badly wounded, with four girls and women raped.

Perhaps most frightening of all, graffiti found at some crime scenes and mutilations suffered by some of the victims indicated to police that they were searching for a devil-worshipper. Even descriptions of the predator were frightening. Survivors sketched a long-faced man with curly hair, bulging eyes, and widely spaced rotten teeth.

Newspapers dubbed him the "Night Stalker."

Fingerprints finally broke the case in August 1985, after police found a car the killer had stolen from his final victim and then dumped. Each person is born with unique fingerprints that leave impressions on most objects handled or touched. Comparison of crime-scene prints to those of potential suspects may narrow a police investigation, but may not qualify as definitive proof of guilt. The prints recovered from it matched criminal records for Richard Ramirez, a 25-year-old drifter from Texas with a history of drug convictions. Relatives told police that Ramirez was obsessed with the song "Night Prowler" by AC/DC—a band whose initials were scrawled at several Night Stalker crime scenes.

Mug shots of Ramirez appeared in newspapers on August 30, 1978. Residents of East Los Angeles spotted him the next day and nearly lynched him before police arrived. In custody, Ramirez boasted of worshipping Satan and told reporters, "I've killed 20 people, man. I love all that blood."

On September 20, 1989, jurors convicted Ramirez of 13 murders and 30 other felonies, recommending death as his punishment. (One case in San Francisco never went to trial.) At his formal sentencing on November 7, Ramirez told the court, "You maggots don't understand me. I am beyond good and evil. I will be avenged. Lucifer dwells in us all."[7]

Despite his appearance and violent behavior, Ramirez attracted a fan club of young women during his trial. One, a self-described Satanist, briefly married Ramirez, while one of his female jurors publicly proclaimed her love for the man she had sentenced to die.

THE "GREEN RIVER KILLER"

One of America's longest-running serial murder mysteries began in January 1982 when police found 16-year-old Leann Wilcox strangled in a field outside Seattle, Washington. Over the next two years authorities blamed an unknown killer for the deaths or disappearances of 48 more victims in the area. Several corpses were pulled from the local Green River, which soon gave the slayer his nickname.

There seemed to be no pattern in selection of the killer's victims, other than the fact that all were female. Ages ranged from 15 years to 36. Most of the victims were Caucasian, but a few were African American. Some worked as prostitutes along the "Sea-Tac Strip," between Seattle and Tacoma, while others were hitchhikers or runaways. A few were never found. Others, who *were* recovered, still are not identified.

Gary Ridgway answers a prosecutor's question during his plea of guilty to 48 counts of aggravated first degree murder in the Green River killing case. *Elaine Thompson/AP*

The crimes frustrated local officers and agents of the FBI who furnished "profiles" of the murderer. While several suspects were investigated and released for lack of evidence, the killings seemed to stop as suddenly as they began. Civilians were relieved, but dedicated officers kept up the search, even when funds were cut and public interest waned.

At last, in September 2001, police officers broke the case.

Gary Leon Ridgway, a Utah native born in 1949, was first questioned as a Green River suspect in March 1986. Detectives searched his home and collected DNA samples from Ridgway in April 1987, but early testing techniques failed to match his DNA with samples obtained from various bodies. That changed in September 2001, when new testing methods matched Ridgway's semen to traces found on four Green River victims.

♀ WHO'S WHO?

Unknown bodies are commonly identified by the same means used for criminal suspects, through fingerprints or DNA profiling. While each person's fingerprints are unique, two-thirds of all humans have prints that form loops, broadly divided as radial (for the

(continues)

Lab workers perform DNA tests at the FBI's state-of-the-art crime lab in Quantico, Virginia. *Charles Dharapok/AP*

(continued)

radius bone in the arm, if they open toward the little finger), or ulnar (for the ulna, if they open toward the thumb). Nearly one-third of all humans have fingerprints featuring whorls, further divided by investigators into plain whorls, double loops, central pocket loops, and accidental loops. A minority of human fingerprints consists of arches, broadly divided into plain and tented varieties.

Special care is needed in fingerprinting corpses, especially if they are burned, badly decomposed, or if they have been submerged in water. Once prints are collected, experts use computers to check them through AFIS—the Automated Fingerprint Identification System—for rapid comparison with prints from known criminals, military personnel, law enforcement officers, and others whose fingerprints are on file with authorities.

When regular fingerprints fail, DNA "fingerprints" may identify a body or a criminal suspect. Forensic scientists examine genetic markers found in bodily fluids or tissues, noting similarities with the DNA collected from a known subject to complete the match. In the case of missing persons, DNA may be collected from various sources (strands of hair on a brush, etc.) for comparison with genetic markers from an unidentified body. When no material from the missing person is available, DNA from family members may prove that the body found belongs to a blood relative.

Police arrested Ridgway in December 2001 on four murder counts, but the list of charges soon lengthened. In April 2002 Ridgway confessed to 25 murders, but even that statement was only the tip of the iceberg. On November 5, 2003, he pled guilty to murdering 48 women. That number included 42 "official" Green River victims, plus six never linked by detectives before 2003. Ridgway received a prison term of life without parole.[8]

Lethal Ladies

On October 9, 2002, Florida prisoner Aileen Wournos died by lethal injection for the confessed murders of six men whom she robbed and shot in random encounters. At her trial in January 1992 Wournos claimed self-defense on her first murder charge, saying that victim Richard Mallory beat and raped her before she shot him. Jurors disbelieved that story, but reporters for NBC's *Dateline* later proved that Mallory had served 10 years in jail for an earlier rape.

By then, it was too late.

Wournos had already confessed to five more murders, saying of those victims, "I just flat robbed and killed them." A second death sentence, imposed for those crimes in May 1992, ensured that she would never leave prison alive.

MEDIA MONSTER

Aileen Wournos (1956–2002) led a tragic life, abandoned by her parents at age four, scarred by burns at age six, and later molested by male relatives. She logged the first of many arrests at 18, including charges of prostitution and theft.

Wournos killed her first known victim in November 1989. Over the next 12 months she shot and robbed at least five more men, most of them "johns" who paid her for sex. (Georgia police suspect Wournos of a seventh killing, which was never charged against her.) Authorities captured Wournos on January 9, 1991, and recovered many items she had stolen from her victims.[1]

Following her execution, Wournos was the subject of a Hollywood film titled *Monster* (2003). Actress Charlize Theron won an Oscar as Best Actress of the Year for her portrayal of Wournos, while some critics claimed that the film made excuses for Wournos's crimes.

DEADLIER THAN THE MALE?

While many media reports called Aileen Wournos the "first female serial killer," they were off by more than 2,300 years. We have already seen that the first serial killers on record, from ancient Rome, were women convicted in 351 B.C. Other examples include

- Margaret Davey, an English cook executed in 1542 for murdering several of her employers
- Marie de Brinvilliers, a French woman executed in 1676 after she confessed to poisoning her father, brothers, lover, and 50-odd hospital patients
- Gessina Gottfried of Germany, beheaded in 1828 for poisoning 20-plus victims over 13 years
- Jane Toppan, a deranged New England nurse who poisoned at least 31 victims (some say 100) between 1880 and 1901, ending her days in a mental hospital
- Lila Young, a Canadian "baby farmer," who killed an estimated 120 infants at her home for unwed mothers, after taking money to place the babies in adoptive homes
- The "Angel Makers of Nagyrev," 26 Hungarian women who mimicked early Roman killers, poisoning dozens of men between 1914 and 1929. All were convicted at trial, with eight sentenced to death.
- The "Angels of Death," four hospital nurses in Vienna, Austria, who murdered at least 42 patients during 1983–89. Police suspect the true body count is closer to 300.

While those cases stand out, they are far from unique. In fact, throughout history, some 12 percent of all identified serial killers are female.[2] The long-standing, mistaken assumption that serial killers are always male probably allowed some female killers to escape detection.

"GENTLE" KILLERS

Some authors describe female serial killers as "gentle" because they rarely use the knives, clubs, and guns preferred by men. Poison is a common lady's weapon, used by 45 percent of the United States'

⚲ FORENSIC TOXICOLOGY

Toxicology is the study of adverse effects caused by various chemicals on living organisms. Poisons are substances that cause injury, illness, or death by chemical reaction. Toxins are naturally occurring substances produced by living cells, such as the bacteria that cause disease. Animal toxins delivered via bites or stings are called *venom*. Poisonous substances cause damage when swallowed or inhaled, while venom is injected by a living creature (but may often be swallowed without injury). Mathieu Orfila, the "father of toxicology," wrote in 1813: "All things are poison and nothing is without poison. It is the dose that makes a thing poisonous."

Three basic types of toxic entities are chemical, biological, and physical. Chemicals include a wide range of inorganic substances (acids, gases, metals) and organic compounds (drugs, medicines, and venoms). Biological toxins include bacteria, parasites, and viruses. Physical toxins include a variety of things normally excluded from lists of poisons, including various forms of light and radiation.

Forensic toxicologists identify poisons and toxins first by observing their victims for characteristic symptoms including rashes, bleeding, paralysis, seizures, hair loss, tissue discoloration, or distinctive odors. (Cyanide emits a smell like bitter almonds.) If no such symptoms are conclusive, various presumptive tests are made, using chemicals known to change color or react in other ways upon contact with various toxins. Tests may often be performed long after death, since some poisons collect in the hair, nails, and other tissues of a victim's body. French emperor Napoleon Bonaparte died in 1821, but tests performed on his hair and clothes in the 1960s found traces of arsenic, prompting some authors to claim he was murdered. Other experts disagree, noting that arsenic was a common part of some nineteenth-century medicines, paint, and dye.

known female serial killers (versus 5 percent of male slayers).[3] Another 32 percent of female killers drown or suffocate their victims, especially children.[4] Both methods are often called "gentle" in comparison to stabbing, beating, or shooting—though the method matters little to their victims.

That difference may explain why so many reporters mistook Aileen Wournos for the first female serial killer. Wournos killed in a "masculine" style, shooting her victims, then stealing and selling their valuables. In fact, however, she was neither the first nor the worst, in terms of methods of slaying victims.

BLACK WIDOWS

Some female serial killers are nicknamed "black widows," after the venomous spiders that kill their male mates upon breeding. (The male counterparts of black widows are "bluebeards," who murder their wives and girlfriends.) While those killers claim a variety of motives, including love and jealousy, a majority murder for money, collecting life insurance or inheritances from their victims.

In fact, a survey of known serial killers worldwide reveals that 41 percent of homicidal women kill for profit, versus 14 percent of male serial killers.[5] That fact, and the absence of clearly recognized sexual motives, may be another reason why female serial killers so often "fly under the radar" where police and journalists are concerned.

Some notorious "black widow" killers include

- Belle Gunness, a nineteenth-century Norwegian immigrant who killed her first husband and two children in Chicago between 1896 and 1900, then moved to an Indiana farm where she invited would-be suitors to visit. Before Belle faked her death and escaped on April 28, 1908, she killed at least 16 more victims, most of them men whom she also robbed. Some sources believe her final body count may exceed 40.
- Vera Renczi, a Romanian who killed two husbands, her son, and 32 lovers in the early twentieth century. She preserved all their bodies in zinc coffins, stacked in her basement.
- Nannie Doss, an American poisoner who in 1955 confessed to 10 murders spanning 31 years. Victims included four husbands,

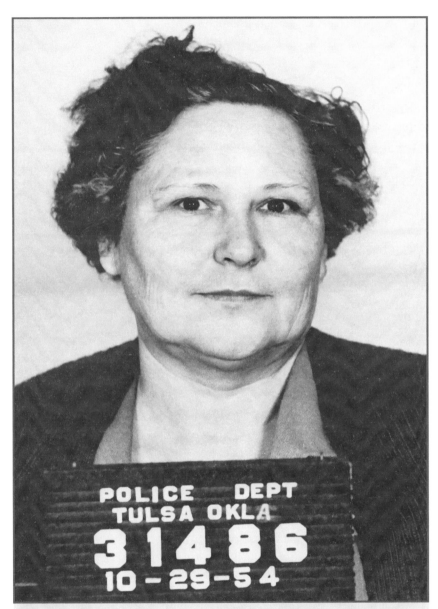

POLICE DEPT
TULSA OKLA
31486
10-29-54

Nannie Doss, a 49-year-old grandmother, is shown in this mugshot taken in Tulsa, Oklahoma, on October 29, 1954. Doss signed statements saying she caused the deaths of four of her five husbands, each in a different state, by putting liquid rat poison in their food and drink. *AP*

"COUNTESS DRACULA"

The strangest and most vicious female serial killer of all time was probably Countess Erzsébet (Elizabeth) Báthory (1560–1614). Born of Hungarian nobility, Báthory grew up in luxury, surrounded by relatives who included kings and knights, judges, bishops, and cardinals. Unfortunately, her bloodline also included strong undercurrents of insanity, alcoholism, sex crimes, and black magic.

It may be no surprise, then, that Erzsébet herself displayed violent, sadistic tendencies from an early age. Married at age 15 to a much older nobleman, she was left alone most of the time with her servants, whom she punished brutally for minor or imaginary offenses. Her several lavish homes included private dungeons and torture chambers, where young maids often spent their last hours in agony.

In Báthory's time the torture and murder of peasants was seldom a crime when committed by nobles. There was, thus, no reason for the countess to restrain herself for fear of punishment. Still, as her reputation spread, Báthory found it hard to replace the servants she killed. Soon, those who remained joined in kidnapping raids for new victims, the better to spare themselves from pain.

four children, and two of her sisters. All left small insurance payments, though Doss insisted that she killed for "true romance."

- Dorothea Puente, an atypical black widow who killed nine male tenants in her Sacramento, California, boarding house between 1982 and 1988. After killing each man, Puente continued to cash his Social Security checks.
- Judias Buenoaño, another profit-motivated slayer who killed her husband, lover, and disabled son for life insurance benefits between 1971 and 1980. Like Aileen Wournos, she was executed in Florida (in 1998).

KILLING FOR ATTENTION

Female serial killers who victimize their own children and other relatives sometimes have a much stranger motive than profit.

By 1610, Báthory's violence was so notorious that King Matthias assigned special investigators to the case. On December 26, 1610, raiders entered Báthory's castle at Csejthe and caught her red-handed, torturing her final victim. The raiders found a diary listing 650 young women whom Báthory had murdered since her marriage in 1575.

While several of her servants were arrested and executed, a special law was passed to permit prosecution of Báthory, who enjoyed the special status of the nobility. Even then, however, she could not be sentenced to death for her crimes. Instead, when convicted, Báthory was walled up inside a wing of her castle, ordered to spend the rest of her life there. Jailers found her dead on August 21, 1614.

Rumors later spread that Báthory tried to stay young by bathing in blood from her victims, but no evidence supports those stories. Still, her crimes inspired a horror film, *Countess Dracula* (1971), in which Ingrid Pitt portrays "Countess Elisabeth Nodosheen" as a real-life vampire.[6] Báthory has also inspired numerous books, video games, and even rock bands.

According to psychiatrists, some of them become addicted to the sympathetic attention they receive after the death of their loved ones.

Munchausen's Syndrome is a form of mental illness named in 1951 for Baron von Munchausen, a legendary eighteenth-century teller of outrageous "tall tales." Victims of Munchausen's Syndrome lie compulsively, concocting stories that bring attention to themselves. Many are extreme hypochondriacs, persons who imagine they are ill and constantly seek treatment for diseases they do not have. In severe cases they may injure or poison themselves to make the conditions seem real.

A similar illness, known since 1977 as Munchausen's Syndrome by Proxy, involves persons who harm others—commonly children—to focus sympathy on themselves. Mothers afflicted with this condition may injure or kill their own children and other relatives or friends in a bid for the attention they receive in hospitals and at funerals. A few famous cases include those of

- Martha Woods, an army wife who murdered four of her own children, plus a nephew, a niece, and a neighbor's child, between 1946 and 1969. Because her family moved frequently, doctors unfamiliar with her history blamed many of the deaths on Sudden Infant Death Syndrome (SIDS). Long afterward, Woods received a life prison term.
- Marybeth Tinning of Schenectady, New York, who lost her first child to legitimate illness in January 1972. Over the next 13 years, she killed eight more children, including one whom she adopted for that purpose. Tinning also claimed harassment by nonexistent stalkers and set her home on fire to prove the point. In 1987 she received a prison term of 20 years to life.
- Diana Lumbrera, another homicidal mother who killed seven of her own children in Kansas and Texas between 1976 and 1990. Separate trials in both states during 1990 resulted in consecutive life sentences.
- Debra Tuggle of Little Rock, Arkansas, who between 1974 and 1982 killed three of her own children and her boyfriend's daughter from a previous marriage. As in other cases, doctors first blamed the deaths on SIDS, then grew suspicious after Tuggle shot herself. She survived that wound, and while jurors convicted her of murder in September 1984, they recommended a lenient 10-year sentence out of sympathy for her mental condition.

Munchausen's cases have caused many doctors to closely examine all cases of SIDS, especially where more than one infant suddenly dies in the same family. Some parents claim that they have been falsely accused of harming their children, but a majority of pediatricians now believe that multiple SIDS deaths within a single family are highly unlikely.

Team Killers

The airborne terrorist attacks of September 11, 2001, claimed nearly 3,000 lives and stunned America. Before that shock had time to dissipate, some persons still unknown mailed deadly anthrax bacteria to members of Congress and other victims, killing more innocent persons. And, as if those crimes were not bad enough, a serial gunman began stalking targets around the nation's capital.

THE "BELTWAY SNIPERS"

Police assumed one shooter was responsible on October 2, 2001, when a rifle shot killed 55-year-old James Martin outside a supermarket in Wheaton, Maryland. One day later, bullets from the same gun killed five more victims and wounded a sixth in six different Maryland cities.

FBI profilers described the sniper as a lone "thrill seeker," but they could not find him and the shootings continued. Between October 7 and 22, in scattered attacks throughout Maryland and Virginia, the same .223-caliber rifle claimed five more lives and left a 13-year-old boy wounded. A note left at the scene of one shooting read: "Dear policeman, I am God."

Two days after the last murder, tips from police in other states led Maryland officers to arrest 41-year-old John Allen Muhammad and 17-year-old Lee Malvo, who posed as Muhammad's son, although they were not related. Investigators and acquaintances from other states linked Muhammad and Malvo to earlier shootings

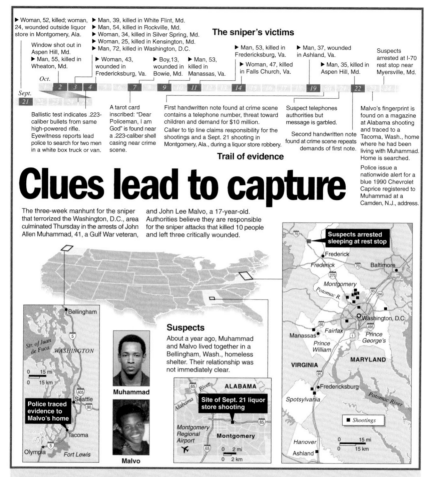

The sniper's victims

- Woman, 52, killed; woman, 24, wounded outside liquor store in Montgomery, Ala.
- Window shot out in Aspen Hill, Md.
- Man, 55, killed in Wheaton, Md.

- Man, 39, killed in White Flint, Md.
- Man, 54, killed in Rockville, Md.
- Woman, 34, killed in Silver Spring, Md.
- Woman, 25, killed in Kensington, Md.
- Man, 72, killed in Washington, D.C.
- Woman, 43, wounded in Fredericksburg, Va.
- Boy, 13, wounded in Bowie, Md.
- Man, 53, killed in Manassas, Va.

- Man, 53, killed in Fredericksburg, Va.
- Woman, 47, killed in Falls Church, Va.
- Man, 37, wounded in Ashland, Va.
- Man, 35, killed in Aspen Hill, Md.

Suspects arrested at I-70 rest stop near Myersville, Md.

Oct.

Sept. 21 — 2 3 4 — 7 — 9 — 11 — 14 — 19 — 22

Ballistic test indicates .223-caliber bullets from same high-powered rifle. Eyewitness reports lead police to search for two men in a white box truck or van.

A tarot card inscribed: "Dear Policeman, I am God" is found near a .223-caliber shell casing near crime scene.

First handwritten note found at crime scene contains a telephone number, threat toward children and demand for $10 million. Caller to tip line claims responsibility for the shootings and a Sept. 21 shooting in Montgomery, Ala., during a liquor store robbery.

Suspect telephones authorities but message is garbled.

Second handwritten note found at crime scene repeats demands of first note.

Malvo's fingerprint is found on a magazine at Alabama shooting and traced to a Tacoma, Wash., home where he had been living with Muhammad. Home is searched.

Police issue a nationwide alert for a blue 1990 Chevrolet Caprice registered to Muhammad at a Camden, N.J., address.

Trail of evidence

Clues lead to capture

The three-week manhunt for the sniper that terrorized the Washington, D.C., area culminated Thursday in the arrests of John Allen Muhammad, 41, a Gulf War veteran, and John Lee Malvo, a 17-year-old. Authorities believe they are responsible for the sniper attacks that killed 10 people and left three critically wounded.

Suspects

About a year ago, Muhammad and Malvo lived together in a Bellingham, Wash., homeless shelter. Their relationship was not immediately clear.

Suspects arrested sleeping at rest stop

Police traced evidence to Malvo's home

Muhammad

Malvo

Site of Sept. 21 liquor store shooting

Graphic shows timeline of shootings and known evidence found in the "Beltway Snipers" case. The maps show the sites of the shootings (right) and the site of the suspects' arrest. AP

in Alabama and the Pacific Northwest. As their confessions soon revealed, authorities had been mistaken: they were looking for *two* killers, all along.

In October 2003 jurors convicted John Muhammad of murder and recommended execution. Lee Malvo received one life prison term in March 2004, and another seven months later. Muhammad

♀ READ ALL ABOUT IT!

Serial murders are sensational crimes, often exploited by the media to sell newspapers and boost TV ratings. Most famous serial killer nicknames—from Cleveland's "Mad Butcher" to the L.A. "Night Stalker"—were thought up by journalists, not by the killers themselves. Rare exceptions—including London's "Jack the Ripper," California's "Zodiac," and New York's "Son of Sam"—were sent by killers to the press, in letters begging for attention.

Media reports may help or hinder a police investigation of serial crimes. Publication of a suspect's description, photo, or license plate number may alert citizens and lead to a criminal's speedy capture. On the other hand, the release of mistaken descriptions produces false leads, while publication of restricted crime-scene details may enable mentally ill persons to deceive investigators with false confessions. Some authorities also complain that lurid media reports create panic and endanger innocent persons, as when a deliveryman in Texarkana, Arkansas, was shot by homeowners frightened of the town's "Moonlight Murderer."

Some killers taunt police and the media by writing letters boasting of their crimes, or predicting new murders to come. This problem dates from 1888, when Jack the Ripper—or, perhaps, someone pretending to be Jack—sent many letters to the newspapers and Scotland Yard. Critics maintain that publishing a killer's letters feeds his evil fantasies, and may provoke "copycat" crimes committed by others. Those who support publication insist that releasing the letters may divert a killer's attention from murder to writing, or that the notes may include unconscious clues leading to the killer's arrest.

There is no doubt that letter-writing killers have inflamed and terrorized some cities, including London, New York, San Francisco, New Orleans, and Wichita, Kansas. The debate continues as to whether such letters are *ever* worth printing, or whether they should be reserved for police and psychiatrists only.

is suspected of three other killings in Alabama and Washington, but no further charges were filed.[1]

MURDER IN TEAMS

While a majority of serial killers act alone, 13 percent of America's solved cases reveal two or more murderers working together. Fifty-six percent of those cases involve two killers acting in tandem, while 44 percent featured three or more slayers.[2]

Further study shows that male pairs are the most common type of serial killing teams, accounting for 30 percent of the total. Male-female couples come next, at 25 percent. All-male "wolf packs," ranging in number from three to six members, account for 10 percent of the total. Larger groups, including homicidal cults, sometimes find male and female killers working together. The rarest type of murder team consists of women only, typically murdering husbands or boyfriends.[3]

While murder is a risky business even for a solo killer, some serial predators apparently derive greater satisfaction from recruiting accomplices and committing their crimes in front of friendly witnesses. Such crimes are often difficult to solve—as in the Beltway Sniper case—because police are trained to think of serial killers as loners. Sadly, that preconception may lead investigators to overlook or misinterpret vital evidence.

KILLING FOR KALI

Kali is the Hindu goddess of creation and destruction. Around the year 1250, a cult of Kali worshipers was organized in India, devoted chiefly to their goddess's destructive side. Known as the Sons of Death, these zealots traveled far and wide, strangling and mutilating travelers they met on rural highways, often robbing those they killed to help support the cult.

Because they posed as innocent religious pilgrims, members of the Kali cult were also labeled *thags* (deceivers). British officers who seized control of India in 1757 called them *thugs*, a term still widely used for any violent criminal.

British control of India did not destroy the Kali cult at first. In fact, cult murders escalated. During 1812 alone, authorities estimated that thugs killed some 40,000 victims nationwide. One thug named Buhram confessed to 931 killings when he was caught in 1840.

By that time, British law was closing in on members of the Kali sect. Between 1830 and 1848, police jailed 4,500 thugs, executing 110 who were convicted of multiple murders. The cult officially disbanded in 1852, but occasional outbreaks continued through the 1860s.

Before he played superspy James Bond onscreen, actor Pierce Brosnan starred in *The Deceivers* (1988), playing a nineteenth-century British tax collector who investigates the thugs and helps bring them to justice.

THE "LONELY-HEARTS KILLERS"

Martha Beck (1920–51) was born with three strikes against her, plagued by a glandular illness that made her grossly overweight, abandoned by her father, and molested by her brother. While working as a nurse, she married at age 22, divorced two years later, and was left with two children whom she could barely support.

In 1947 she met Raymond Fernandez (1914–51), a sweet-talking con artist who romanced lonely women, then robbed them and moved on to his next conquest. At first, he planned to swindle Beck, but they soon became lovers and partners in crime.

Thereafter, Martha posed as Raymond's sister, making him seem more respectable to his potential victims. And while Fernandez had never been violent, Beck proposed that in the future they should leave no witnesses alive to testify in court.

Beck and Fernandez killed their first known victim, Myrtle Young of Chicago, in August 1948. Over the next seven months, they killed at least two more women and one victim's two-year-old daughter. Some authors suggest a much higher death toll, but evidence to support additional killings is lacking.

Police caught on to the "Lonely Hearts Killers" when a friend of one missing victim grew suspicious. She privately investigated their background, tracing Beck and Fernandez to a rented house in Queens, New York. There, investigators found a corpse beneath the basement's brand-new concrete floor.

At trial, both defendants claimed insanity, but jurors convicted them and recommended death. Beck and Fernandez appealed that verdict to the U.S. Supreme Court, which rejected their pleas for mercy. Both were executed at New York's Sing Sing Prison on January 2, 1951—Beck after eating a double helping of chicken, potatoes, and salad.

Two decades later, a film depicting the couple's crime spree—*The Honeymoon Killers* (1970)—starred Shirley Stoler as Martha Beck and Tony Lo Bianco as Ray Fernandez. As usual for Hollywood, it mingled fact and fiction in pursuit of a sensational result.

A DEADLY "FAMILY"

Charles Manson is another felon whose grim childhood may help explain his crimes, but it does not excuse them. Born in 1934, the son of an unmarried teenage prostitute, Manson was left with relatives at age five when his mother went to prison for robbery. A cruel uncle sent Manson to school dressed as a girl in hopes of teaching Manson to "act like a man."

Trouble followed, including a series of arrests that placed Manson in custody, where he was beaten and molested by guards and older juveniles alike. Convicted on federal auto-theft charges in 1955, Manson drifted in and out of prison for the next 12 years, finally released—over his own objections—during 1967's psychedelic "Summer of Love."

Manson soon lost himself in San Francisco's "hippie" scene, taking any drugs available, flirting with Satanism, and collecting younger runaways into a loose-knit group he called "The Family." The group, ranging at various times from a dozen to 30-odd members, drifted up and down the California coast, living by theft, drug sales, and sidewalk begging. Finally, in 1968, the Family turned to murder.

Homicide investigators disagree on Manson's final tally of victims. Los Angeles prosecutor Vincent Bugliosi, who sent Manson and several of his followers to death row in 1970, estimates that the group killed at least 36 persons between August 1968 and November 1969, but no charges were filed in most of those cases.[4]

Manson's most notorious crimes occurred on August 9-10, 1969. In two successive nights of gruesome violence, the killer cult claimed seven victims in Los Angeles, including actress Sharon Tate and coffee heiress Abigail Folger. Testimony at trial convinced jurors that Manson hoped to start a race war in America by killing

Convicted serial killer Charles Manson in 1986. *AP*

wealthy whites and blaming the murders on African Americans. After the war, he claimed, survivors would rally to him in the California desert and accept his leadership.

Things never got that far for Manson and his Family. One of his killers, Susan Atkins, was arrested on a minor charge and bragged about the murders to her cellmates. Soon, police jailed Manson, Atkins, and six others who were convicted and sentenced to death in a series of trials during 1970–71. None were executed, however, since the Supreme Court overturned prevailing death penalty laws in 1972, automatically commuting all capital sentences across the country to life imprisonment.

Still, Manson and his "children" kept making news. Family-related murders continued during 1972–73, while some of Manson's girls conspired with neo-Nazis in a foiled prison break. In September 1975 Manson follower Lynette "Squeaky" Fromme tried to assassinate President Gerald Ford, but her pistol misfired.

♀ THE "HILLSIDE STRANGLERS"

Angelo Buono (1934–2002) and Kenneth Bianchi (1951–) had much in common. Both were children of broken homes, addicted to sexual violence. Both hated women. And, like nineteenth-century killers Micajah and Wiley Harpe, they were cousins. Buono moved from New York to California with his mother in 1939, later compiling a record of juvenile arrests. Bianchi followed in 1976, by which time Rochester police suspected him of killing three young girls.

In Los Angeles the cousins reunited for a brutal murder spree that claimed 10 lives during 1977–78. Together, they snatched young women, and then tortured and killed them, leaving their bodies exposed on hillsides and freeway on-ramps. Police initially believed those crimes were the work of one man, whom reporters nicknamed the "Hillside Strangler." The lone-killer assumption confused psychological profilers and led police to dismiss eyewitness reports of *two* suspects sighted near various crime scenes.

After their tenth murder together, in December 1978, Bianchi got nervous and fled to Bellingham, Washington, but his old urges soon returned. In January 1979 he killed two more young women, to whom he had offered a housesitting job. Friends of the victims reported that link to police, and Bianchi confessed to the crimes.

But he had more to say.

In a bid to avoid execution, he gave up cousin Angelo for the Hillside murders and agreed to testify in court. Bianchi later changed his mind, but jurors still convicted Buono on nine murder counts, in November 1983. He died in prison on September 21, 2002. Cousin Ken, meanwhile, remains in a Washington state prison.[5]

Manson, meanwhile, remains an object of fascination for journalists ranging from local reporters to Geraldo Rivera. In 1999 Manson volunteered to teach a legal class at California's Newman University. As he told the press on that occasion, "I have 50 years of experience in incarceration. I pretty much have a leg up on the law from an underworld perspective."

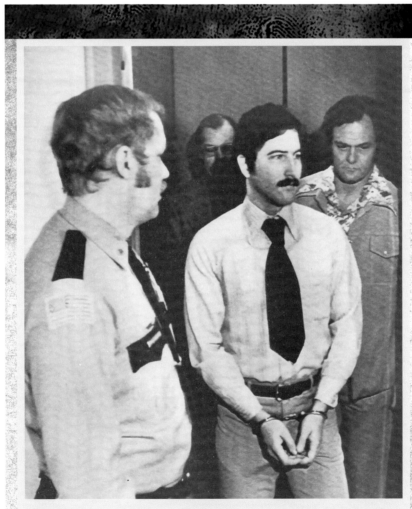

Kenneth Bianchi, center, is escorted from an elevator to a courtroom in Bellingham, Washington, for arraignment on a stolen property charge on January 19, 1979. At this time, he was being questioned in the "Hillside Strangler" case. *AP*

6

Bad Medicine

In February 1983 a special grand jury convened in San Antonio, Texas, to investigate the deaths of 47 children at a local hospital during 1978–82. At the same time, another panel in neighboring Kerr County investigated eight children's deaths at a local clinic. Police believed the children were killed with overdoses of a muscle-relaxing drug. Their prime suspect was a nurse, Genene Ann Jones.

A DEADLY HEALER

Born in 1950, Jones was a former beautician who entered nursing at age 27, working at several San Antonio-area hospitals over the next five years. In 1982 she joined Dr. Kathleen Holland in private practice, but bad luck followed her.

Seven children suffered unexplained seizures under Jones's care in August and September 1982, climaxed by the death of 15-month-old Chelsea McClelland. Dr. Holland fired Jones on September 26, while investigators looked into her background. They soon found a trail of mysterious deaths spanning Jones's entire medical career.

Police named Jones as a suspect in 10 murders, but she only faced charges for killing Chelsea McClelland and drugging four-week-old Roland Santos (who survived). Evidence in many other cases was destroyed when hospital administrators prematurely shredded 9,000 pounds of records related to Jones's employment. Because hospital records were destroyed, the suspicion against Jones in most of her alleged crimes could not be pursued in any depth.

At trial in January 1984, prosecutors claimed that Jones poisoned children in order to pose as a "hero" by saving their lives, though some died when she failed to revive them. A second motive seemed to be a scheme for boosting business for the clinic where she worked by making children ill.

Convicted of murder in February 1984, Jones received a 99-year prison term. Eight months later, she got another 60 years for poisoning Roland Santos. Some authorities believe she killed most of the 55 children lost on her watch in two counties, but no further charges were filed.

MEDICAL MURDER

While all doctors and nurses swear an oath to "do no harm," some still wind up killing or injuring their patients through some criminal activity. Such crimes are often difficult to prove because so many people die in hospitals and rest homes from disease or major injuries.

♀ "DOCTOR DEATH"

Dr. Harold Shipman (1946–2004) presently holds the record as England's worst serial killer. He may also be the world's most prolific medical murderer, with 215 victims confirmed and many more suspected. His motive, say police, was pure greed.

Shipman studied medicine at Leeds University, where classmates deemed him "a bit strange," and entered practice at Todmorden, Yorkshire, in March 1974. A year later, his partners discovered that Shipman was stealing (and using) drugs from the office. They fired him and informed police, who fined Shipman $1,000 for forging prescriptions.

Despite that scandal, Dr. Shipman found new partners at Hyde, in September 1977, and then set up shop on his own with some 3,000 patients in 1992. Sadly for those who trusted him, Shipman's main interest was money, not healing the sick.

Between 1992 and 1998, Shipman persuaded patients to donate some $34,000 for new medical equipment, while others named him as a beneficiary in their wills. One patient, Kathleen Grundy, left Shipman $675,000 when she died at age 82, in June 1998—a circumstance that naturally made her relatives suspicious.

Between 1965 and 1992, police and FBI agents investigated eight hospitals in the United States, alleging that 192 patients were murdered while under medical care. No defendants were convicted in those cases, although one suspect in Maryland surrendered her nursing license. During the same period (1980–81), Toronto's prestigious Hospital for Sick Children suffered 43 infant deaths in which poisoning was suspected but never proved.

Overall, 5 percent of America's identified serial killers belong to medical professions—doctors, dentists, nurses, or hospital aides. Some are sadists who target helpless patients, but the FBI's *Crime Classification Manual* also suggests more unusual motives. [1]

Some medical slayers, when caught, describe their crimes as "mercy" killings, meant to end the suffering of patients near death or in serious pain. Others, like Genene Jones, seek to pose as "heroes" by saving the lives of patients whom they, themselves,

Police began investigating Shipman's practice, quickly noting its high patient-death rate. Three months after Grundy's death, authorities charged Shipman with her murder, and they soon exhumed more patients to examine their remains for evidence of deadly drugs.

The search paid off.

On January 31, 2000, jurors convicted Britain's "Dr. Death" of killing 15 patients with overdoses of pain medication between 1993 and 1998. He received a life prison term, but the worst revelations still lay ahead.

In July 2000 police suggested that Shipman might have murdered 192 patients. Ten months later, detectives speculated that Shipman had killed at least 297 victims, perhaps 345. Judge Janet Smith, speaking in July 2002, blamed Shipman for 215 slayings, while listing another 200 deaths as "highly suspicious."

Dr. Shipman's true tally may never be known. On January 13, 2004, guards at Wakefield Prison found Shipman hanging in his cell. Investigators ruled his death a suicide.

placed at death's door.[2] In either case investigators must look closely to determine whether certain deaths in hospitals and rest homes are as "natural" as they appear.

CRUEL "MERCY"

One self-described mercy-killer who nearly got away with it was Donald Harvey, a nurse's aide who murdered numerous patients between 1970 and 1985. Although sentenced to prison for 37 murders—thus breaking the official U.S. record previously held by John Wayne Gacy Jr.—Harvey convinced police of his guilt in 50 more slayings.

A longtime mental patient and self-described Satanist, born in 1952, Donald Harvey landed his first job at a Kentucky hospital at age 18, in May 1970. Over the next 15 years, he worked at five other hospitals in Kentucky and Ohio. Dozens of patients died under Harvey's care, including 23 in the last 13 months before his final arrest.

Doctors and hospital administrators knew that Harvey was "peculiar." In 1972 he spent two months in mental hospitals, receiving 21 electroshock-therapy treatments. In July 1985 he was jailed for bringing a pistol and other contraband items to work at a Cincinnati veterans hospital, but another hospital in the same city hired him seven months later. After his murder conviction, an Ohio hospital administrator pled guilty to faking death records for some of Harvey's victims, hoping to save the hospital from lawsuits.

Suspicion fell on Harvey in early 1987 when a medical examiner autopsied one of his patients and smelled the odor of almonds—an indicator of cyanide poisoning. The subsequent investigation led to Harvey, whom police charged with one count of murder in March 1987. Over the next few months, he cheerfully confessed to the "mercy" killings of that victim and 86 others. Harvey's confessions, including admission of many deaths that were deemed natural, were crucial because many relevant hospital records had been destroyed.

In August 1987 Harvey pled guilty to 25 Ohio murders, receiving four life prison terms. A month later, he admitted to nine Kentucky slayings and received eight more life terms plus 20 years. Finally, in February 1988, he pled guilty to three more Ohio killings and three attempted murders.

Still, despite the shocking scope of Harvey's crimes, other medical killers are suspected of much worse.

"DOUBLE-O SWANGO"

Dr. Joseph Michael Swango first fell under suspicion of killing his patients in 1983, but police had great difficulty proving their case. Over the next 16 years he dodged investigators on two continents, becoming one of the world's most notorious medical killers. In fact, so many patients died in Swango's care after routine examinations

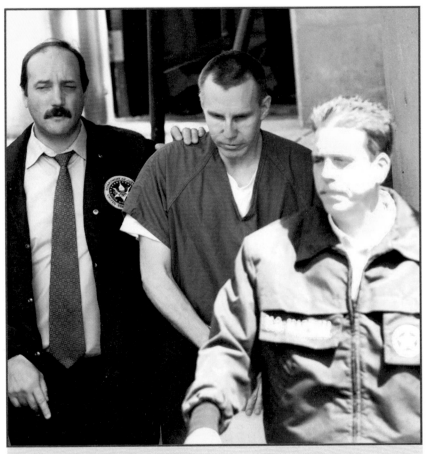

Dr. Michael Swango being led out of the federal courthouse.
M. McLoughlin/N.Y. Post/Corbis Sygma

that his colleagues dubbed him "Double-0 Swango," after fictional spy James Bond's "double-0" license to kill.

Swango was born in 1954, in Tacoma, Washington. His teachers ranked him as a genius in high school, with an I.Q. of 160, and the National Merit Scholarship organization called him "High School Student of the Year" in 1975. Eight years later, Swango received his medical degree from Southern Illinois University.

But something was wrong with Dr. Swango. Officials at Ohio State University (OSU) expelled him from the school's internship program in June 1984, after seven of his patients died under suspicious circumstances. (Twenty-six years later, Swango confessed to murdering patient Cynthia McGee at OSU.)

Swango moved on to become an emergency medical technician for an Illinois ambulance company, where police arrested him in October 1984 on charges of poisoning his coworkers with arsenic. They all survived, but Swango received a five-year prison term for aggravated battery and Illinois revoked his medical license.

Released on parole in August 1987, Swango forged various documents to mask his criminal record, claiming he was jailed for a barroom brawl. A South Dakota hospital hired him in July 1992, and then fired him five months later, after learning the true facts of his case. Moving on, Swango conned his way into a New York residency program in June 1993. Five more of Swango's patients died before New York officials recognized his lies and fired him, four months later.

In 1994 Dr. Swango surfaced in Zimbabwe, Africa, working at Mnene Hospital. Administrators there suspended Swango on July 21, 1995, after two of his patients were poisoned. Undeterred by the latest setback, Swango promptly applied for a hospital job in Saudi Arabia. While waiting for an answer to that application, he spent a year hiding in Zambia and Europe.

The Saudi hospital accepted Swango, but before moving on to the Middle East, he flew to Chicago on June 27, 1997. FBI agents met him at the airport, arresting him on charges of practicing medicine without a license and falsifying various documents during 1987–93. Swango finally pled guilty on those charges and received a 42-month prison term in June 1998.

Next, in July 2000, a federal grand jury indicted Swango for killing three patients at a New York veterans hospital. He pled guilty to those charges on September 6, 2000, and received a sentence of life imprisonment without parole. His subsequent confession to one murder in Ohio left the official tally at four victims, but police speculate that Swango killed at least 35 persons worldwide—and perhaps many more, still unidentified.

Chamber
of Horrors

America was a kinder, gentler country in the 1920s, before the Great Depression and Second World War. Some residents of New York City even trusted total strangers with their children in those days. On May 27, 1928, Edward and Delia Budd welcomed a man who called himself Frank Howard to their flat on West 115th Street. Howard had responded to an ad placed in the *New York World* by their teenage son, seeking a summer job. The Budds prepared lunch for their visitor and tried to make him feel at home.

Howard was middle aged, well dressed, and courteous. They talked about his small farm on Long Island, where Edward Jr. would spend the summer working. Throughout the meal and conversation, Howard complimented 12-year-old Grace Budd on her fine manners and good looks, surprising Ed and Delia when he suddenly invited Grace to join him at a birthday party being given for his niece that afternoon.

The Budds were hesitant at first, but Howard laid their fears to rest. His niece lived with her family nearby, he said, around the corner of Columbus and 137th Streets. It was an easy walk, and Howard would return Grace to her parents by late afternoon. Worried that Howard might retract his job offer if they refused, the Budds agreed. They stood together, on their doorstep, watching as Grace and Frank Howard walked off hand-in-hand.

The Budds never saw Grace again.

By nightfall they were worried, but police could offer little help. The party was a hoax, they quickly learned—in fact, Columbus Avenue ran only to 110th Street. There was no farm, no Frank

Howard, on Long Island. Crime reports revealed that Howard matched descriptions of a "Gray Man" who had snatched at least three other children from the streets of New York City, but his true identity remained unknown.

Albert Howard Fish sits on a courthouse bench. Fish claimed to have abused 400 children across the United States, killing as few as eight and as many as 15. *Murray Becker/AP*

Grim days turned into weeks, then months and years. The Budds had given up all hope by mid-November 1934, when they received an unsigned letter in the mail. Its author claimed to be a cannibal whose taste for human flesh developed on a trip to China during 1894. In closing, he described Grace's abduction in detail and claimed that he had killed her and then devoured her remains.

Police suspected that the letter was a cruel, sick joke, but they proceeded to investigate. The envelope bore a crossed-out symbol of the Private Chauffeurs' Benevolent Association (PCBA), headquartered in Manhattan. Detectives soon identified a PCBA janitor who took some of the envelopes and later left them at his former boarding house on East 52nd Street, in Room 11. There, landlady Frieda Schneider identified the current occupant of Room 11 as Albert H. Fish. Officers arrested Fish on December 13, removing several razor blades from his pockets.

In custody, the 64-year-old suspect surprised police by confessing to Grace Budd's murder and various others, starting with the slaying of a Delaware man in 1910. Most of his victims were children, whom Fish molested at every opportunity. Prosecutors accused Fish of abusing at least 100 children in 23 states, while Fish himself claimed 400 victims from coast to coast. He had killed at least eight of those victims, Fish said, perhaps as many as 15.

At trial for Grace Budd's murder, Fish filed an insanity plea. Psychiatrists reported that he suffered from religious mania and constantly tortured himself, inserting dozens of needles into his own flesh. X-rays confirmed that fact, but prosecution experts countered with claims that Fish was evil, not insane.

Jurors convicted Fish of first-degree murder on March 22, 1935. Sentenced to die, Fish lost all appeals and kept his date with New York's electric chair on January 16, 1936. According to one witness, the chair malfunctioned on its first attempt, needing a second jolt of electricity to finish off the job.

BAD OR MAD?

Insanity is a legal concept, unrelated to medical diagnosis of mental illness. From 1843 through the early 1970s, most U.S. states defined insanity as the inability to tell right from wrong or to act in compliance with the law. Criminals who took steps to conceal their crimes were therefore "sane," no matter how outrageous or demented their behavior.

Today, some states permit a plea of "diminished capacity" (similar to the old insanity rule) or "guilty but mentally ill," which permits a sentence of confinement in a mental hospital, with psychiatric treatment, until experts agree a defendant is safe for return to society.

The question of insanity is often left for juries to decide, though most jurors have no medical training and naturally fear returning dangerous criminals to the streets. That fear increases when a defendant confesses to multiple violent crimes such as murder or rape.

Ironically, while the crimes of many serial killers appear to be acts of insanity, very few are found to be legally insane. Over the past century, only 2 percent of the United States' known serial killers have escaped trial on grounds of mental illness, while about 1 percent of those facing trial were acquitted on grounds of insanity (and confined to psychiatric hospitals).[1] Some fake insanity, but nearly all are convicted and sentenced to death or to long prison terms. Just as one is considered innocent until proven guilty, defendants are considered sane unless they can prove otherwise. Still, no system is perfect, as our next case demonstrates.

THE CO-ED KILLER

Edmund Kemper III was the product of a broken home; his mother criticized him constantly and locked him in the basement as punishment for minor acts of disobedience. By age 10, Kemper showed a fascination with death, killing family pets and mutilating his sister's dolls. At 14, in August 1963, he murdered both of his maternal grandparents on their California ranch. A judge deemed Kemper insane and confined him to a mental hospital until age 21.

In 1969, ignoring objections from Kemper's psychiatrists, state authorities released Kemper to his mother's custody. By then he was a giant, six feet nine inches tall, weighing 300 pounds. Despite ongoing psychiatric therapy, Kemper began killing again in May 1972, while living with his mother in Santa Cruz. Over the next nine months he murdered and dismembered six co-eds (female college students), whom he met while they were hitchhiking. Finally, on Easter weekend, Kemper killed his mother and one of her female friends at home, and then fled to Colorado, where he stopped and called police from a roadside telephone booth. He confessed and waited for local officers to come pick him up.

Kemper's confession, like that of Albert Fish, included claims of cannibalism and other bizarre activities suggesting an unstable mind. Jurors, recalling his seven years of wasted psychiatric

⚲ EDWARD GEIN (1906–1984)

No American serial killer has had greater impact on Hollywood than Edward Theodore Gein (rhymes with green). Over the past half-century, his ghoulish crimes have inspired no less than four

(continues)

A police officer examines the junk-littered kitchen in the farm house of Edward Gein, where authorities found human skulls and other parts of human bodies. They also found the butchered body of Bernice Worden hung in a shed near the house. *Bettmann/ Corbis*

(continued)

novels and 10 motion pictures. Young viewers know him by other names: as Norman Bates in *Psycho* and its sequels, as "Leather-face" in the *Texas Chainsaw Massacre* films, or as "Buffalo Bill" in *The Silence of the Lambs*. And yet, Gein's crimes were more bizarre in some respects than anything displayed on movie screens.

A semi-recluse, Gein lived with his mother on a farm outside Plainfield, Wisconsin, until she died in 1945. Thereafter, his obsession with death and female anatomy ruled Gein's life. He began robbing graves in 1947, taking body parts to decorate his farmhouse and himself. Somewhere along the way, he also started killing to collect fresh specimens. In November 1957 Gein shot Bernice Worden at her Plainfield hardware store and carried her away. Evidence from the crime scene led police to Gein, who had left a receipt for antifreeze on the checkout counter. Earlier in the day, he'd told Worden's son that he was going to town to buy antifreeze, and the son made the connection. At Gein's home, police found remains of at least a dozen corpses. Some clearly came from old graves, while other bits had never been embalmed.

Gein confessed to two murders—Mrs. Worden's and that of Mary Hogan, in December 1954—but trial judge Robert Gollmar blamed Gein for at least four more slayings. Police charged him with two murder counts, but the court ruled him mentally unfit for trial in January 1958, confining him to Central State Hospital. His trial proceeded in November 1968, and Judge Gollmar found Gein innocent by reason of insanity. Gein returned to the asylum, where he died on July 26, 1984.

Gein's shocking crimes prompted unknown arsonists to burn his home in March 1958. They have since become one of the darkest episodes in American legend.

treatment, found Kemper sane and convicted him on eight murder charges. When the judge asked Kemper to suggest a proper punishment, Kemper replied, "Death by torture." Instead, he received a sentence of life imprisonment—with possible parole.

"THE DIE SONG"

Curiously, at the same time that Ed Kemper stalked young women in Santa Cruz, another serial killer also terrorized the same city. Born in 1947, Herbert Mullin was voted "most likely to succeed" by his high school classmates, but drugs and depression drove him into a mental institution at age 23. The treatments he received did not silence the voices in his head that urged Mullin to kill. Convinced that California was about to suffer massive earthquakes, Mullin believed he could prevent the disaster with a series of human sacrifices, committed while chanting a tune he called "the Die Song."

Between October 1972 and February 1973, Mullin claimed 13 victims around Santa Cruz, including a priest who heard his confession at St. Mary's Church. Between Mullin's crimes and those of Ed Kemper, Santa Cruz briefly earned the unwelcome nickname of "Murderville, USA." Police arrested Mullin on February 6, after witnesses to his last crime saw his car's license plate, and jurors later convicted him on 10 counts of murder. Like Kemper, Mullin received a life prison term. He is eligible for parole in 2020.

THE ZOMBIE-MAKER

Future serial killer Jeffrey Dahmer suffered sexual abuse by a neighbor at age eight, shortly before his parents divorced. Two years later, in 1970, he began secretly "experimenting" with dead animals. In June 1978, soon after his high school graduation, Dahmer picked up a male hitchhiker, invited him home for drinks, then beat and choked the stranger to death.

That crime apparently shocked Dahmer back to his senses—at least, for a while. He tried college but quit, then joined the army for a six-year term and was discharged after two years for heavy drinking. Dahmer settled in Wisconsin, where police arrested him for indecent exposure in 1982, and again in 1986. In the second case he received a suspended jail sentence with orders for psychiatric counseling.

It didn't help.

Between September 1987 and July 1991, Dahmer murdered 16 boys and young men at his Milwaukee apartment, sometimes

Herbert Mullin, 25, is shown leaving court in Santa Cruz, California, after being arraigned on charges of killing six people. He was later charged and convicted for the first degree murder deaths of four teenagers who were each shot in the forehead at their mountain campsite. *AP*

devouring parts of their bodies, building a shrine with their skulls. As detailed in his later confession, Dahmer was obsessed with the idea of making "zombies" who would serve him as slaves. To that end, he drilled holes in his living victims' skulls and doused their brains with chemicals, but none survived.

Local police missed two chances to interrupt Dahmer's reign of terror. In January 1989 he received a one-year jail term for molesting a teenage boy, but officers missed the evidence of murder at Dahmer's apartment. He served 10 months and emerged from prison to kill the live victim's brother in May 1991. That victim briefly escaped Dahmer's clutches, nude and bleeding from head wounds,

Police surround the apartment of serial killer Jeffrey Dahmer in Milwaukee, Wisconsin. *AP*

but policemen who answered the report of a disturbance accepted Dahmer's claim that the incident was a "lover's quarrel." They left the boy to Dahmer and his fate.

Two months later, another victim fled Dahmer's home with handcuffs dangling from his wrist. This time, police searched Dahmer's flat and found the remains of 11 victims. Charged with 15 counts of murder, Dahmer filed a plea of "guilty but insane" in January 1992. Jurors disagreed and convicted him on all counts, resulting in a minimum sentence of 936 years. In prison, Dahmer refused all offers of protective custody. A fellow inmate beat him to death on November 28, 1994. Dahmer's killer proclaimed himself the "son of God," stating that he had acted upon his "father's" commands.

Still at Large

On August 16, 1938, workers clearing a garbage dump in Cleveland, on Lake Erie, found two dismembered human bodies. The man and woman, killed about four months apart, were the twelfth and thirteenth victims of a serial slayer known only as the "Mad Butcher of Kingsbury Run." Police had no clues to the killer's identity—and he was not finished, yet.

A MODERN HEADHUNTER

Part of the Butcher's first victim, an unidentified woman, washed ashore on Cleveland's Euclid Beach in September 1934. Over the next six years, police found 15 more mutilated corpses, several dumped in a downtown railroad gully called Kingsbury Run, which gave the killer his media nickname. Of those 15 victims, only three have been reliably identified.

While many serial killers stalk victims who resemble one another, Cleveland's Mad Butcher killed 10 men and six women, 14 Caucasians and one African American. Two bodies were treated with an unknown chemical preservative. Ten of the severed heads were never found, suggesting they were kept as grisly souvenirs.

America's Great Depression (1929–41) retarded identification of the Butcher's victims. During that period millions of homeless people drifted around the country, seeking work. The victims could have been from anywhere. Those finally identified were traced through fingerprints, because all three had criminal records.

Eliot Ness, made famous as characterized in *The Untouchables*, was Cleveland's public safety director during the Butcher's reign of terror. In pursuit of the Butcher, police questioned known associates of the killer's three identified victims, posted photos of the

A poster from Eliot Ness's unsuccessful run for mayor of Cleveland in 1947. Ness investigated the murders attributed to the "Mad Butcher of Kingsbury Run." *Piet Van Lier/AP*

unidentified dead in a vain effort to learn their names, and grilled various known sex offenders in Cleveland. Ness also teamed detectives with city fire inspectors, thereby allowing them to search various buildings without standard warrants, but they never found the killer's presumed "laboratory." Long afterward, Ness claimed that he had confronted the killer in autumn 1938, prompting the Butcher to seek refuge in a mental hospital, where he allegedly died in 1941. However, that theory fails to explain how the Butcher returned to kill three more victims, found together in May 1940. And if that riddle was not daunting enough, a seventeenth body surfaced in Cleveland on July 23, 1950. Longtime medical examiner Samuel Gerber, who examined most of the Butcher's victims, reported that the latest corpse's mutilation "resembles exactly" the Mad Butcher's style.

THE ONES WHO GET AWAY

A global survey of serial murder cases since 1900 reveals that 18 percent—nearly one in five—remains unsolved today.[1] Experts offer various reasons for that frightening statistic: traveling killers who claim victims over widespread areas, slayers who disguise their crimes as natural deaths, or "linkage blindness"—a term coined by Dr. Steven Egger, describing police failure to link crimes in a series. According to Dr. Egger, linkage blindness occurs when officers in various police departments fail to communicate regarding unsolved crimes in different jurisdictions. The problem increases when two or more departments are actively antagonistic to each other—or to federal investigators. Clues, connections, and suspects are thus overlooked, allowing killers to remain at large and active.

Whatever the reason, notorious (though unknown) serial killers have eluded police throughout recorded history. A few examples include

- The "Servant Girl Annihilator," blamed for eight murders in Austin, Texas, during 1884–85
- The "Toledo Clubber," slayer of six Ohio victims from 1925 to 1926
- "The Doodler," who killed 14 gay men in San Francisco during 1974–75, leaving sketches of his victims

The "From Hell" letter written to George Lusk from Jack the Ripper.
Enclosed with the letter was half of a human kidney preserved in
wine. It was received October 16, 1888. *Alen MacWeeney/Corbis*

- The "Southside Slayer," blamed for killing 14 women in Los Angeles between 1983 and 1987
- The "Highway Killer," linked to the deaths of nine women around New Bedford, Massachusetts, in 1988
- The "Independence Avenue Killer," responsible for 13 deaths in Kansas City during 1996–97

While DNA and other forensic tools help police identify many more killers today than in the past, without a suspect for comparison, no evidence has much value.

"JACK THE RIPPER"

Between August and November 1888, a serial killer nicknamed "Jack the Ripper" killed and mutilated five women in London, England. All of the victims were prostitutes, murdered and left on display as if to shock society. While many killers have claimed more victims, Jack still ranks among the most notorious. According to the judges on TV's *Jeopardy*, more books, articles, plays, and movie scripts have been written about the Ripper than any other murderer in history, except Adolf Hitler.

Jack the Ripper got his nickname from a series of letters sent to police and the press while his crimes were in progress. One letter included half of a human kidney, possibly taken from one of the Ripper's victims—though several authors believe medical students mailed it as a prank. Today, some experts believe that most—if not all—of the letters were fakes, but others disagree, citing particular notes to support their theories of the killer's true identity. Debate also continues over the final tally of Jack's victims, some estimates ranging as high as 20, but London's police insist that only five were legitimate Ripper slayings.

What makes Jack the Ripper so popular with crime writers and readers? First, he may have been the earliest to taunt authorities with letters boasting of his crimes.

But more importantly, he got away with it.

Over the past 120 years, various authors have named many Ripper suspects, citing "evidence" that ranges from DNA and handwriting samples to pure speculation. Some of the better-known suspects include

- Montague Druitt (1857–88), a London lawyer who committed suicide soon after the Ripper's last crime, leaving a note that voiced fears for his own sanity
- Severin Klosovski (1865–1903), a barber hanged for killing his three wives, suspected as the Ripper by several London detectives
- Prince Albert Victor Christian Edward (1864–92), heir to the throne of England, linked to the Ripper slayings in various conspiracy theories published since 1962

♀ "THIS IS ZODIAC SPEAKING"

Between 1966 and 1969 an unknown killer claimed at least six lives in California, leaving two other victims badly wounded. Like the Texarkana murderer of 1946, he sometimes struck in lover's lanes. As in the Ripper case from 1888, police and journalists received a string of taunting letters, some of them in code. In California, though, authorities agreed that most of those grim

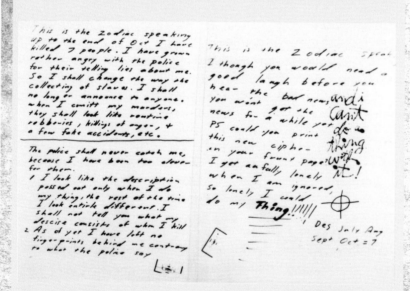

One of the infamous Zodiac killer's letters, written in 1969.
Bettmann/Corbis

- Walter Sickert, a British artist first named as a suspect in 1976. Twenty-six years later, novelist Patricia Cornwell allegedly matched Sickert's DNA to a "new" Ripper letter, but critics remain unconvinced.

The most recent Ripper film, *From Hell* (2001), stars Johnny Depp as a policeman who investigates a government conspiracy to cover up the Ripper's crimes and spare Prince Albert from exposure of his secret marriage to a commoner.

messages were truly written by the killer who called himself "Zodiac."

Cheri Bates was the slayer's first victim, stabbed to death at Riverside City College the night before Halloween, 1966. The killer penned his first letter days later, telling reporters: "Bates had to die. There will be more."

And so there were.

From December 1968 through October 1969, the Zodiac used San Francisco and its environs as his private hunting ground, shooting and stabbing three couples, and finally killing a cab driver in his taxi. Each time, new letters offered details of the crimes known only to police and to the killer. After the final shooting, officers received a bloody portion of the taxi driver's shirt.

While the Zodiac's confirmed murders stopped in 1969, he kept writing letters—21 in all—through April 1978. Police and private investigators have named at least seven Zodiac suspects, most notably Arthur Leigh Allen, a convicted sex offender who allegedly bragged of committing the crimes.

Police questioned Allen repeatedly and searched his home in February 1991, but he died in August 1992 without any charges being filed against him. Despite public accusations, handwriting experts declared in 1971 that Allen did not write the Zodiac letters. Likewise, DNA testing performed in October 2002 proved that Allen did not lick any stamps or envelopes linked to the Zodiac's taunting correspondence.[2]

"THE AXEMAN'S JAZZ"

Between August 1910 and October 1919, a brutal home-invader terrorized New Orleans, Louisiana, chiseling through doors and wield-
ing an axe against victims sleeping in their beds. The raids left 11
persons dead and eight wounded, while thousands more barred their
doors and slept with weapons close at hand.

In the midst of that panic, on March 14, 1919, a local newspaper
published a letter signed by "The Axeman," demanding that every
home should play jazz music on March 19—St. Joseph's Night—or face
the killer's wrath. "One thing is certain," the letter said, "and that is
that some of those people who do not jazz it will get the axe!"

That March 19 was noisy in New Orleans, including widespread
performances of a song called "The Axeman's Jazz," composed especially for the occasion. The killer claimed no victims on St. Joseph's
night, but two more fell before the crime spree ended, as mysteri-
ously as it had begun.

Unlike the Ripper's case in London, two suspects were tried and
convicted for one Axeman slaying, the death of a young girl slain on
March 10, 1919. The child's mother, Rose Cortimiglia, named two
neighbors as the killers. Jurors believed her, although her husband
testified for the defense, but she later recanted her story and the
defendants went free.

Meanwhile, police and writers speculated on the timing of the
crimes, including a six-year gap between murders in 1912 and 1918,
suggesting that the killer may have been in jail during those years.
In 1953 author Robert Tallant published the story of suspect Joseph
Mumfre, allegedly killed in Los Angeles by the widow of an Axeman victim on December 2, 1920. Mumfre supposedly served prison
time for burglary during the Axeman's break from killing, and that
seemed to solve the case.

In truth, however, evidence uncovered by researcher William
Kingman in 2001 reveals that no person named Joseph Mumfre died
in Los Angeles—or anywhere else in California—during the twentieth century.[3] Since Tallant died in 1957, we cannot ask where he
got his story, but today we know that it was false.

MURDER BY MOONLIGHT

Like most Americans, residents of Texarkana—a town divided by
the Texas-Arkansas border—celebrated the end of World War II

and a return to peace in August 1945. That welcome peace was shattered six months later by a serial killer who stalked couples in lover's lanes and in their homes, striking at three-week intervals, always attacking by the light of a full moon.

Texarkana's "Moonlight Murderer" let his first two victims live, in February 1946, but the abuse they suffered was so vicious that 19-year-old Mary Larey begged the masked gunman to kill her. Thereafter, between March and May, the stalker fatally shot five victims and wounded a sixth, leaving no useful clues but a flashlight dropped at the final crime scene.

Local police and Texas Rangers hunted the killer in vain, some officers dressing as women to park with their "boyfriends" in hope that the slayer would come within range of their guns. Nervous residents shot at their neighbors and hapless delivery boys, but thankfully, no one was killed in the crossfire.

Two days after the killer's last attack, on May 6, 1946, police found a man's mangled body on the railroad tracks outside Texarkana. Reporters speculated that the killer had committed suicide, but stab wounds on the corpse marked Earl McSpadden as another murder victim. Whether Texarkana's moonlight stalker or some other enemy killed him, no one can say with certainty.

A film about the Texarkana case, *The Town That Dreaded Sundown* (1977), depicts a shootout with police that left the wounded killer with a limp, but no such event occurred in real life. Despite the naming of a local car thief as a suspect in the case, the lead investigators still consider it unsolved.

A Worldwide Problem

Police in Rostov, Russia, faced a serious problem in the 1980s. Their city was home to a vicious serial killer who kidnapped girls and boys alike from local railroad depots, but detectives had no clue to his identity. In fact, they could not even admit he existed.

According to the tenets of Soviet communism, Russia's conversion to a socialist state in 1917 had created a "worker's paradise," in which no major crimes occurred. Because the existence of a "Western-type" killer embarrassed communist leaders, police could only search for him secretly, without warning the public. So it was that the search took 10 years and cost 53 lives.

THE ROSTOV RIPPER

Andrei Chikatilo (1936–94) was a late-blooming serial killer who claimed his first victim at age 42. He later blamed his crimes on the trauma of seeing his brother killed and eaten by starving neighbors in the late 1930s, but if true, his rage took 40 years to surface.

Before he turned to murder, Chikatilo was a teacher, but he lost his job when students charged him with molesting them. Demoted to work as a traveling salesman, Chikatilo brooded over the "injustice" of his treatment, and in time surrendered to his secret urges, which included cannibalism.

Russian police framed an innocent man for Chikatilo's first murder and put him to death, but the near-miss failed to deter Chikatilo from killing again. Between 1981 and 1990, he slaughtered

Andrei Chikatilo, also known as "The Butcher of Rostov," sits in his prison cell. Convicted of 52 murders, he was executed on February 15, 1994. *Epix/Corbis Sygma*

52 more victims—eight in August 1984 alone—and spread a pall of terror over Rostov. Police questioned Chikatilo, along with 25,000 other suspects, but Communist Party officials intervened to have him released.

Meanwhile, detectives working on the case caught 95 other killers and 245 rapists, proving once and for all that the communist system was not free of crime.

Chikatilo's luck ran out in November 1990, when police saw him at a Rostov railway station with bloodstains on his face and hands. While they did not arrest him at the time, they noted his name and remembered two weeks later, when his last victim was found nearby.

Finally arrested on November 20, Chikatilo confessed to 53 murders. Jurors convicted him on 52 counts in October 1992, and he received a death sentence. After various appeals, he was executed on February 15, 1994.

A WORLD OF PREDATORS

While offenders in the United States account for 85 percent of all serial killers so far identified, such crimes have never been restricted to the United States.[1] As we have seen, ancient Rome spawned the first known serial killers, and modern innovations in forensic science have helped to identify notorious predators around the world. Their number includes

- Daniel Barbosa, the slayer of 72 young girls in Colombia and Ecuador between 1974 and 1988
- Kampatimar Shankariya, a resident of India, convicted of 70 murders in 1979
- Gennadiy Mikhasevich, a Russian executed in February 1988 for the murders of 33 women since 1973
- Jose Rodriguez Vega, a Spaniard who killed 16 elderly women during 1986–88
- Anatoly Onoprienko, a Ukrainian nicknamed "The Terminator," who robbed and killed 52 victims in their homes during 1989–96
- Ahmad Suradji, an Indonesian "wizard" who sacrificed 42 women in black-magic rituals, between 1986 and 1997
- Moses Sithole, South Africa's worst serial killer so far, with 38 victims confirmed during 1995
- Huang Yong, slayer of 23 victims in China's Henan Province during 2001–03

As terrible as those crimes were, they pale beside the acts of others who murdered 100 victims or more.

THE "MONSTER OF THE ANDES"

Pedro Alonzo Lopez was born at Tolima, Colombia, in 1949, the seventh of 13 children from an unmarried prostitute. He arrived during *La Violencia*, a bloody era (1946–58) that saw some 200,000 Colombians killed in guerrilla warfare.

Lopez ran away from home after a teacher molested him, and he suffered more abuse in prison as a teenager, while serving time for auto theft. In custody, he killed three older convicts who assaulted him, and jailers called the slayings self-defense.

Released a short time later, Lopez embarked on a horrific odyssey of rape and murder spanning the nations of Colombia, Ecuador, and Peru. His victims were girls, many of whom he snatched from rural villages. As Lopez later explained his crimes to police, "I lost my innocence at age eight, so I decided to do the same to as many young girls as I could."

Ecuadorian villagers captured Lopez in April 1980 and delivered him to police. Far from denying his crimes, Lopez readily confessed to 300-plus murders. According to his statement, Lopez had killed 100 girls in Colombia, at least 110 in Ecuador, and "many more than 100" in Peru.

Police were skeptical of such claims until Lopez led them to the graves of 53 victims around Ambato, Ecuador. As one police spokesman told reporters, "If someone confesses to 53 you

♀ "A SERIAL KILLER'S PLAYGROUND"

Ciudad Juarez, Mexico, lies just across the border from El Paso, Texas. Many of its two million residents work in factories that operate 24 hours a day, turning out cheap clothes and other items made for export to America. In 2003 Amnesty International reported that 370 young women had been murdered in and around Ciudad Juarez since 1993.

Most of those crimes remain unsolved today.

Reporters call Juarez a "serial killer's playground."

No one suggests that one man is responsible for all the murders in Ciudad Juarez. In fact, since 1996, Mexican prosecutors have convicted 12 defendants in 27 of the killings. Nine other suspects—including eight former policemen—are listed as fugitives, linked to the murders of 10 local victims.

The charges filed against police have encouraged speculation that other officers may be involved in the killings, or that they may have suppressed evidence. Other popular theories include drug syndicates killing female employees who "know too much," Satanic cults performing human sacrifices, and black-market organ harvesters. In 2004 Mexican authorities announced plans to prosecute 18 cases of illegal trafficking in human organs, but none have yet been tried in court.

find and hundreds more you don't, you tend to believe what he says."

Newspapers dubbed Lopez the "Monster of the Andes." The *Guinness Book of World Records* called him the world's most prolific serial killer (before Harold Shipman), but his punishment was relatively light. Convicted of 57 murders in Ecuador, Lopez received a life prison term—but he was paroled and deported to Colombia in 1996. At last report, he was still free, living under a new name, at an unknown address.

"EL LOCO"

Pedro Lopez aside, Colombia remains one of the world's most violent nations. In 2002 a total of 28,837 persons were murdered

Theories aside, one thing is clear in Ciudad Juarez: Despite international protests, the murders continue. No woman is safe on the streets of the serial killer's playground.

Family and friends of women slain in Ciudad Juarez carry photos of some of the 370 victims in the Mexican city since 1993.
Eduardo Verdugo/AP

nationwide, for an average rate of 78 murders per 100,000 residents.[2] (The United States, with a population more than six times the size of Colombia's, has a murder rate of only 4.6 per 100,000.) In 2005 Colombia claimed the world's second-highest murder rate, after South Africa.[3]

While Colombia's "normal" murders usually involve drugs or politics, some crimes still shock police despite the nation's bloody history. During the 1990s, an unknown killer stalked children in the Colombian Andes, claiming dozens of victims between Bogotá and Pereira. Police jailed a known child-molester in December 1998, but the murders continued while he was in custody, forcing investigators to release him.

In April 1999 officers arrested 42-year-old Luis Garavito for attempted rape, and he surprised them by confessing to the murders of 140 children whom he listed in a small notebook. Garavito—known to his friends as *"El Loco"* (The Madman)—claimed a motive similar to that of Pedro Lopez, citing molestation and abuse during his childhood. After suffering that trauma, he explained, "I became a monster. There was a superior being inside me."

By October 1999, police said Garavito had directed them to bodies of 114 victims, kidnapped from 60 towns in 11 of Colombia's 32 provinces. Two months later, officials raised the tally to 182, including children killed in Ecuador. During 2000, 11 separate trials sentenced Garavito to 835 years in prison, but Colombian law dictates that no prisoner may serve more than 60 years.

"A BEAST, NOT A MAN"

On December 2, 1999, police in Lahore, Pakistan, received a startling letter. Its author, Javed Iqbal (1961–2001), confessed to killing 100 boys and dissolving their bodies in acid at his home, located 200 yards from police headquarters. "In terms of expense," Iqbal wrote, "including the acid, it cost me 120 rupees [$2.40] to erase each victim."

Police knew Iqbal as a chemist indicted three times for child-molestation in the 1990s (but never convicted). After receiving his letter, they rushed to his home, but Iqbal was gone. Instead, they found partial remains and belongings of 69 victims.

Officers soon jailed four friends of Iqbal, teenagers Zafar Ahmed, Muhammad Sabir, Shahzad Sajid, and one known only as Nadeem.

Iqbal surrendered on December 30, after granting a newspaper interview to explain his motives.

According to Iqbal, his crimes were acts of revenge against policemen who beat him after one of his previous arrests. "I was so badly beaten," he said, "that my head was crushed, my backbone broken, and I was left crippled. My mother cried for me. I wanted 100 mothers to cry for their children. I could have killed 500, but the pledge I had taken was of 100 children, and I never wanted to violate this."

Iqbal initially repeated his confession in court, while Muhammad Sabir admitted strangling one victim himself. Then, at trial in February 2000, Iqbal recanted his confession, blaming "20 friends of mine" for the murders. Prosecutors disagreed, telling the court that Iqbal was "a beast, not a man."

On March 16, 2000, Judge Allah Ranjah convicted Iqbal of 100 murders, Sajid of 98, Nadeem of 13, and Sabir of three. Iqbal and Sajid were sentenced to death, later reduced on appeal to life imprisonment. On October 8, 2001, jailers found Iqbal and Sajid hanging in their cells. Their deaths were officially described as suicide.

The Mindhunters

"Mindhunters"—the psychological profilers who describe unknown felons from evidence found at their crime scenes— have attained near-mythic status in America over the past quarter century. Author Thomas Harris blazed the trail with his novel *Red Dragon* (1981) and its sequels, *The Silence of the Lambs* (1988) and *Hannibal* (1999). Other novelists with successful profiler series of their own include Alex Kava, James Patterson, Michael Slade, and Robert Walker.

Hollywood, meanwhile, has elevated profiling to an almost supernatural talent, portraying FBI agents whose psychic flashes help them identify serial killers in films such as *Manhunter* (1986), *The Silence of the Lambs* (1991), and *Red Dragon* (2002), or in TV series such as *UNSUB* (1989), *Millennium* (1996–99), and *Profiler* (1996–2000).

Real-life profilers, now retired—John Douglas, Roy Hazelwood, Robert Ressler, and others—often support that impression of amazing success in their published memoirs. But how true-to-life are those stories, in print or onscreen?

CLASSIFYING KILLERS

Far from being any kind of psychic gift, profiling is a matter of research and educated guesswork. Beginning in the 1980s, members of the FBI's Behavioral Science Unit—now called Investigative Support Services—interviewed dozens of notorious killers in prison, collecting information on their backgrounds and motives, and their selection of victims and methods of murder. The end result was a system of classifying killers, based on how they think and operate, as organized or disorganized.

Organized offenders typically rank above average in intelligence and social skills, often holding a skilled job or profession as adults. Frequently, they are the first-born children in their families. Most live with a partner as adults and display no serious sexual problems. Their violence is fueled by stress, sometimes by alcohol or drugs.

Organized killers plan their crimes in advance, often targeting strangers, and take all steps possible to hide or destroy evidence. Their crimes may involve elements of fantasy and ritual, repeated time after time as a kind of signature. Because they take such care in planning and concealing crimes, organized slayers may go on killing for years, undetected (like John Gacy Jr.), or may never be caught at all (like Cleveland's "Mad Butcher").

Disorganized killers are the exact opposite of organized offenders, frequently displaying lower-than-average intelligence. They have few, if any, friends or lovers. Their crimes are impulsive, often committed on a whim, with no planning or serious effort to hide evidence. They rarely kidnap or torture victims, preferring a sudden "blitz" attack on the spur of the moment. Most, like Wisconsin's Edward Gein, are caught through careless errors of their own that lead police to their doorsteps.

FBI agents soon realized that their system of classification was not complete. They added a third category for mixed offenders, whose methods vary from one crime to another. Ted Bundy is a prime example, carefully hiding the bodies of his early victims, and later going on a rampage in a public place that left police with ample evidence to convict him.

Retired profilers often boast of their success in tracking serial killers, but caution is needed when reading such claims. It is true that some FBI profiles—like those of "Sacramento Vampire" Richard Chase and Florida "Want-Ad Killer" Bobby Joe Long—prove eerily accurate with suspects in custody, but few lead directly to an arrest. Chase, for instance, was caught at a busy shopping mall while wearing bloody clothing from his last crime. Long was arrested after he released his last victim alive, to summon police.

In order to evaluate mindhunting fairly, we will now examine two famous cases that reveal profilers at their best, and at their worst.

♀ JOHN DOUGLAS (1945–   )

Former FBI agent John Douglas is America's best-known "mind-hunter," familiar to millions from his best-selling books and frequent appearances on TV talk shows. In 1983 he suffered a near-fatal stroke while visiting Seattle to investigate the infamous Green River murders. In 1997 the parents of JonBenét Ramsey hired Douglas as part of their effort to prove they did not kill their daughter. Between those events, Douglas served as the model for "Agent Jack Crawford" in *The Silence of the Lambs*.

Unlike fictional FBI agents, Douglas and his team did most of their profiling work at the FBI Academy in Quantico, Virginia, rarely visiting a crime scene. His job involved reviewing crime scene evidence and photographs, using statistics and personal insight to suggest an unknown killer's sex, race, age, occupation, and motive.

Douglas profiled hundreds of unsubs during his 18 years at Quantico (1977–95), and his various books—*Mindhunter* (1995), *Journey into Darkness* (1997), *Obsession* (1998), etc.—commonly present profiling as a great success. In fact, when all the details of a case are analyzed, we find that many profiles *are* remarkably accurate . . . but they rarely, if ever, produce an arrest. For all the hard, conscientious work of agents like Douglas and his successors, it remains for local police to collect evidence and link it to a suspect.

SUCCESS: THE "MAD BOMBER"

Between November 1940 and December 1956, an unknown "mad bomber" planted 30 explosive charges in public places around New York City. Most were small bombs, and some failed to explode, but several persons were hurt in the later blasts, between 1953 and 1956. The bomber left notes at his crime scenes, signed "F. P.," often attacking the Consolidated Edison power company.

After 16 years, police still had no clues to the bomber's identity. In December 1956 they asked a local psychiatrist, Dr. James Brussel, to prepare the first official profile of an unknown subject (*unsub* in

FBI jargon). Brussel examined the bomber's letters, concluding from his handwriting and messages that the unsub was a middle-aged white male of Slavic origin, a Catholic, single, and living in Connecticut with an unmarried female relative. He was paranoid, and had a bitter grudge against Con Edison. Incredibly, Brussel even predicted that when detectives found the bomber, he would be wearing a double-breasted suit with the jacket buttoned.

At Brussel's suggestion, police examined Con Edison's employee records, where they found a file on George Metesky, employed by

Psychiatrist Dr. James A. Brussel holding a copy of his book, *Casebook of a Crime Psychiatrist*. Dr. Brussel created the first official criminal profile of an unknown subject in an attempt to catch the "mad bomber" that terrorized New York City between 1940 and 1956. *Bettmann/Corbis*

the company from 1929 to 1931. After an accident at work, Metesky had complained of headaches, but Con Ed's management later fired him and denied him a disability pension. When detectives interviewed him at the Connecticut home he shared with his two single sisters, Metesky wore a double-breasted suit with the jacket buttoned!

In custody, Metesky (1903–94) freely confessed to the bombings, explaining that the "F.P." signature on his letters stood for "Fair Play." A judge found Metesky insane and committed him to the Matteawan State Hospital, where he remained under treatment until 1973. He committed no more crimes and died peacefully two decades later.

Dr. Brussel's profile of the Mad Bomber remains the most astounding real-life example of mindhunting in history. No other profiler has rivaled Brussel's feat—and some profiles, as we shall see, are worse than useless.

FAILURE: THE "SKID ROW SLASHER"

In Los Angeles, between December 1964 and January 1975, a knife-wielding stalker killed and mutilated 11 homeless men ranging in age from 43 to 67. Reporters dubbed him the "Skid Row Slasher." A 10-year gap between the first two murders and the later nine suggested that the killer might have been in prison for some other crime during that period.

On January 31, 1975, police published a psychological profile of the Slasher, including an artist's sketch. Profilers described the unsub as a Caucasian male in his late 20s or early 30s, six feet tall and 190 pounds, with shoulder-length blond hair and some visible (but unspecified) deformity. They called him a gay, friendless loner and a "sexually impotent coward, venting his own feelings of worthlessness on hapless derelicts and down-and-outers."

That profile apparently angered the Slasher, since he killed his last victim—43-year-old Clyde Hay—later the same afternoon.

Police finally caught the Slasher by chance, when he changed his methods to invade a Hollywood apartment on February 2, 1975. Frightened off by a tenant, the prowler dropped a letter addressed to himself in the driveway of a next-door neighbor, movie star Burt Reynolds. Detectives arrested suspect Vaughn Greenwood and searched his home, finding cufflinks stolen from a Slasher victim killed in January.

The problem: Although 32 years old and gay, Greenwood was African American, with no deformity of any kind.

Prosecutors charged Greenwood with 11 murders in January 1976. At trial, 12 months later, jurors convicted him on nine counts and he received a life prison term. A separate trial added 32 years for assault on two victims who survived the Slasher's attacks.

VICAP VS. VICLAS

In May 1985 the FBI introduced its computerized Violent Criminal Apprehension Program (VICAP), designed to link unsolved crimes by collecting signature details from thousands of cases nationwide. To make VICAP work, local homicide detectives must fill out questionnaires describing every detail of a crime and submit the form to FBI headquarters for analysis.

Many officers resented the extra paperwork, even when VICAP's report form was shortened from 44 pages to 15. If a killer claimed 20 victims, they complained, the FBI still demanded 300 pages of information on top of the many reports detectives already must file for their own agencies. And, in fact, while VICAP has proved useful in linking certain unsolved crimes, no killers have been caught by the system after 22 years online.

Canadian investigators launched a new program—the Violent Crime Analysis Linkage System (ViCLAS)—in December 1993. ViCLAS also requires investigators to complete a questionnaire, 83 items vs. VICAP's 189, and by December 1995, it had warned police that Canada harbored 20 active serial killers. Today, homicide investigators in Australia, Austria, China, and Sweden, as well as several U.S. states, use ViCLAS.

FBI agent Mike Cryan, assigned to VICAP, has called ViCLAS "the Cadillac system in the world," while VICAP pioneer David Cavanaugh (at Harvard University) said: "The Canadians have done to automated case linkage what the Japanese did with assembly line auto production. They have taken a good American idea and transformed it into the best in the world."[1]

But does case linkage *solve* crimes? Most detectives still prefer old-fashioned police work, including collection of fingerprints, blood samples, and other evidence from crime scenes. While DNA databanks have proved their usefulness in catching criminals, profiling still remains more magic than science for many investigators.

Solving Serial Crimes

Investigation of serial murders is serious business. In "normal" homicide cases, where a killer targets a personal enemy for private reasons, the suspect may be obvious—and even if not captured, he or she may never strike again. Serial killers, by contrast, may be lifelong predators, threatening everyone around them, and many take great care to cover their tracks.

STEP ONE: IDENTIFYING MURDER

In any homicide case, police must first determine if a murder has occurred. Some killings, however tragic, are simple accidents or may be justified by law (as in a case of self-defense). First-degree murder requires a criminal intent to kill, without any justification or other excuse (such as intoxication or mental illness) that may reduce degrees of guilt.

Some crime scenes without a body present may appear to represent a murder, but homicide investigators must satisfy themselves and a court of law that a death has occurred before any suspects are convicted of murder. Corpses are not required to prove a case, however, when persuasive evidence—large amounts of blood, a victim's otherwise unexplained disappearance, etc.—demonstrates that a known individual clearly suffered fatal injuries.

STEP TWO: IDENTIFYING VICTIMS

While some murderers—including a few serial killers—have been convicted without corpses, and many were imprisoned for killing unnamed victims, it is virtually impossible to charge a suspect for murdering a victim whose name is unknown and whose body is missing. Either a body or a name is thus essential to a homicide investigation.

Identifying victims may also help police identify their killers. Once a victim is known, detectives can question his or her relatives, coworkers, friends, and enemies, reconstructing the victim's movements and contacts prior to death. Most U.S. homicide victims are slain by someone they know, and while serial killers often break that pattern, tracing a victim's activities may still provide useful links.

Did the victim often spend time at a particular mall, gym, bar, or restaurant? Did he or she hitchhike? Did the victim have a risky job, or one that led to frequent contact with strangers? Do friends and relatives recall the victim mentioning a new friend or lover? Did the victim complain of being stalked or harassed?

Each link presents police with opportunities to locate suspects or important witnesses, including some who may be unaware that what they've seen is vitally important to the case.

STEP THREE: CONNECTING CRIMES

By any definition, regardless of the number cited by a particular source, serial crimes involve repeated offenses, often called "pattern" or "signature" crimes because they strongly resemble one another. Serial killers often abduct, torture, kill, and dispose of their victims in the same way, time after time. Some often or always take "trophies"—a piece of clothing or jewelry, perhaps—which marks the crime as a particular killer's handiwork.

Where a killer preys on victims in one neighborhood or city, police generally recognize pattern elements in the crimes. This is especially true if multiple victims are killed with the same (or the same kind of) weapon. Some officers resist admitting that a serial killer is active in their jurisdiction, while others may withhold details from the media for security reasons, but sooner or later, the pattern reveals itself.

Recognition of related crimes may take longer with nomadic killers who leave victims scattered—or, worse yet, concealed—in widely separated places. Police in different states or cities may not have occasion to discuss their separate unsolved crimes with one another. In such cases, submission of crime-scene details to VICAP or ViCLAS computer analysts may provide the missing links and permit coordination of investigations throughout the country or around the world.

STEP FOUR: IDENTIFYING SUSPECTS

Careless killers help police identify them by leaving crucial evidence—fingerprints, footprints, DNA samples, or teeth marks—at various crime scenes. Even so, that evidence is only useful if investigators have a suspect who matches the clues, either in person or through some database of samples kept on file.

Without those links, police rely on witnesses who may have seen a suspect or a vehicle that may become a focus of investigation. Failing that, authorities sometimes rely on psychological profiles to narrow down the type of suspect they are seeking. As noted earlier, profiles may help or hinder the police, depending on their accuracy.

A recent breakthrough in DNA technology permits forensic scientists to chart the ancestry of an unknown subject from blood, hair, or other biological traces. Thus, authorities may narrow their search to suspects whose great-grandparents were Asian, Hispanic, and so forth—more information, in fact, than the killer may possess about himself!

Finally, though, apprehension of any offender requires old-fashioned police work—tracing leads; questioning witnesses, victims and suspects; checking addresses and former employers; and locating vehicles, weapons, and other vital pieces of evidence.

STEP FIVE: CAPTURE!

Arresting a serial killer is dangerous work. While such offenders often seem mild-mannered to their friends and neighbors, they are deadly, often skilled with weapons, and have no reluctance to kill or injure other people. Some resist violently, forcing police to use deadly force, while a few (like Joe Ball in Texas) kill themselves to avoid punishment.

Still, surprisingly, a majority of serial murder suspects revert to meek behavior when confronted by police. Some even seem pleased that their nightmare is over. A sizeable number confess their crimes, plead guilty at trial, and are packed off to prison without complaint.

Indeed, authorities find that some serial killers go overboard with confessions, claiming "credit" for crimes they did not commit—and for some that never occurred. In 1983 crime partners Henry Lucas and Ottis Toole confessed to 365 murders, including some for which other suspects were already serving life terms. Today, though both men ultimately died in prison, journalists and prosecutors still debate who committed some of those crimes, some believing that the real killers are still at large.

Chronology

331 B.C.	*Rome:* Authorities convict 170 women of poisoning "countless" men.
70 A.D.	*Rome:* Defendant Asprenas tried for killing 130 victims.
1090–1272	The Assassins cult murders victims throughout the Middle East and Europe.
1440	*France:* "Bluebeard" Gilles de Rais executed for killing more than 100 children.
1611	*Hungary:* Countess Erzsébet Báthory imprisoned for murdering 650 young women.
1719	*Italy:* Female defendant La Tofania executed for poisoning 600 victims.
1790s	*Ohio/Kentucky:* Cousins Micajah and Wiley Harpe terrorize travelers along the Wilderness Trail.
1830–1848	*India:* British authorities convict 4,500 Thugs, including 110 charged with multiple murders.
1872–1873	*Kansas:* The "Bloody Benders" kill and rob at least a dozen travelers at their roadside inn.
1880	*New England:* Nurse Jane Toppan poisons the first of an estimated 100 patients.
1888	*London:* "Jack the Ripper" eludes arrest after killing five women.
1893	*Chicago:* Herman Mudgett builds his "murder castle," victimizing visitors to the World's Fair.
1897	*France:* Joseph Vacher executed for killing 14 victims.
1908	*Indiana:* Belle Gunness escapes after killing an estimated 28 victims at her farm.
1924	*Poland:* Cannibal-killer Karl Denke hangs himself in jail while awaiting trial for 31 murders.
1925	*Germany:* "Hanover Vampire" Fritz Haarmann executed for 24 murders.

1929	*Hungary:* Authorities convict 26 women—the "Angel Makers of Nagyrev"—for poisoning numerous husbands and lovers.
1934–1938	*Cleveland:* An unknown "Mad Butcher" dismembers at least 16 victims.
1936	*New York:* Cannibal Albert Fish executed for one of 15 suspected murders committed since 1910.
1957	*Wisconsin:* Grave-robber Edward Gein charged with two murders, suspected of several more.
1957–1958	*Nebraska:* Teenage lovers Charles Starkweather and Caril Fugate claim 11 victims.
1961	German author Siegfried Kracauer coins the term *serial murder.*
1962–1964	*Boston:* The "Boston Strangler" claims 11 female victims. DNA evidence later invalidates the 1967 confession of suspect Albert DeSalvo.
1969	*Los Angeles:* Charles Manson's "family" kills seven celebrity victims.
1973	*California:* Juan Corona convicted of killing 25 migrant workers.
1976–1977	*New York City:* David "Son of Sam" Berkowitz terrorizes the borough of Queens with nocturnal shootings.
1976–1977	*Los Angeles:* "Hillside Stranglers" Kenneth Bianchi and Angelo Buono murder 10 women.
1977–1980	*U.S.A.:* Racist gunman Joseph Paul Franklin claims at least 20 victims in seven states.
1980	*Chicago:* John Wayne Gacy Jr. convicted of 33 murders and sentenced to death.
1980	*South America:* "Monster of the Andes" Pedro Lopez confesses to killing 310 children in three countries.
1983	*Texas:* Henry Lucas and Ottis Toole confess to 365 murders, some of which are later disproved.
1985	*Washington, D.C.:* The FBI's Violent Criminal Apprehension Program (VICAP) goes online.
1989	*Florida:* Theodore Bundy executed for one of his 30 confessed murders, spanning the U.S. in 1974–76.

1989 *Mexico:* Police find 25 bodies at a Matamoros ranch occupied by drug-cultist Adolfo Constanzo.

1990 *Vienna:* Austrian prosecutors convict four nurses of killing 15 hospital patients.

1991 *Los Angeles: Silence of the Lambs* wins five Academy Awards, including Best Picture of the Year.

1992 *Milwaukee:* Jeffrey Dahmer convicted of 17 murders.

1993 *Canada:* The Royal Canadian Mounted Police launch their Violent Crime Analysis Linkage System (ViCALS).

1993–2004 *Mexico:* 370 young women die at the hands of unknown killers in Ciudad Juarez.

1994 *Russia:* Andrei Chikatilo executed for 52 murders committed between 1978 and 1990.

1996 *California:* William Bonin executed for 10 "freeway murders" committed during 1979–80.

1998 *China:* Bai Baoshan executed for 15 serial murders.

1999 *Colombia:* Luis Garavito confesses to killing 182 children.

1999 *Ukraine:* "Terminator" Andrei Onoprienko convicted of killing 52 victims since 1989.

1999 *Pakistan:* Javed Iqbal confesses to murdering 100 boys.

2001 *Washington, D.C.:* "Beltway Snipers" Lee Malvo and John Muhammad terrorize the nation's capital.

2003 *China:* Huang Yong executed for 25 murders.

2003 *Seattle:* Gary Ridgway pleads guilty to 48 murders committed since 1982.

2004 *England:* Dr. Harold Shipman, suspected slayer of 297 patients, hangs himself in prison.

Endnotes

Chapter 1

1. John Douglas, Ann Burgess, Allen Burgess, and Robert Ressler, *Crime Classification Manual* (San Francisco: Jossey-Bass, 1992), 20–21.
2. Michael Newton, *The Encyclopedia of Serial Killers*, 2d edition (New York: Facts on File, 2006), 238.
3. Ibid., 140.
4. Ibid., 185–6.
5. David Lester, *Serial Killers* (Philadelphia: Charles Press, 1995), 126–160.
6. Douglas et al., *Crime Classification Manual*, 20–21.
7. Newton, *The Encyclopedia of Serial Killers*, pp. 272–3.

Chapter 2

1. Newton, *The Encyclopedia of Serial Killers*, 116.
2. Ibid.
3. Ibid.
4. Ibid.
5. Ibid.

Chapter 3

1. Terry Sullivan and Peter Maiken, *Killer Clown* (New York: Grosset & Dunlap, 1983).
2. Clifford Linedecker, *The Man Who Killed Boys* (New York: St. Martin's, 1980).
3. David Abrahamsen, *Confessions of Son of Sam* (New York: Columbia University Press, 1985).
4. Maury Terry, *The Ultimate Evil* (New York: Doubleday, 1987).
5. Anne Rule, *The Stranger Beside Me* (New York: Signet, 2001).
6. Stephen Michaud and Hugh Aynesworth, *Ted Bundy: Conversations with a Killer* (New York: New American Library, 1989).
7. Clifford Linedecker, *Night Stalker* (New York: St. Martin's, 2004).
8. Carlton Smith and Thomas Guillen, *The Search for the Green River Killer* (New York: Onyx, 1991).

Chapter 4

1. Dolores Kennedy and Robert Nollin, *On A Killing Day* (Chicago: Bonus Books, 1992).
2. Newton, *The Encyclopedia of Serial Killers*, 286.
3. Ibid.
4. Ibid., 280.
5. Ibid., 286–7.
6. Raymond McNally, *Dracula Was A Woman: In Search of the Blood Countess of Transylvania* (New York: McGraw-Hill, 1987).

Chapter 5

1. Sari Horwitz and Michael Ruane, *Sniper: Inside the Hunt*

for the Killers Who Terrorized the Nation (New York: Random House, 2003).
2. Newton, *The Encyclopedia of Serial Killers*, 253.
3. Ibid.
4. Vincent Bugliosi and Curt Gentry, *Helter Skelter* (New York: Norton, 1974).
5. Ted Schwartz, *The Hillside Strangler* (New York: Doubleday, 1981).

Chapter 6
1. Douglas et al., *Crime Classification Manual*.
2. Douglas et al., *Crime Classification Manual*, 111–122.

Chapter 7
1. Newton, *The Encyclopedia of Serial Killers*, 176–7.

Chapter 8
1. Newton, *The Encyclopedia of Serial Killers*, 263.
2. Ibid., 302–6.
3. Ibid., 10–11.

Chapter 9
1. Newton, *The Encyclopedia of Serial Killers*, 95–6.
2. Ibid.
3. Ibid.

Chapter 10
1. Newton, *The Encyclopedia of Serial Killers*, 271–2.

Bibliography

Apsche, Jack. *Probing the Mind of the Serial Killer.* Morrisville, Penn.: International Information Associates, 1993.

Douglas, John, Ann Burgess, Allen Burgess, and Robert Ressler. *Crime Classification Manual.* San Francisco: Jossey-Bass, 1992.

Douglas, John, and Mark Olshaker. *Mind Hunter.* New York: Scribner, 1995.

Egger, Steven. *Serial Murder: An Elusive Phenomenon.* New York: Praeger, 1990.

Everitt, David. *Human Monsters.* Chicago: Contemporary Books, 1993.

Fido, Martin. *A History of British Serial Killing.* London: Carlton Books, 2001.

Frasier, David. *Murder Cases of the Twentieth Century.* Jefferson, N.C.: McFarland, 1996.

Godwin, Grover. *Hunting Serial Predators.* Boca Raton, Fla.: CRC Press, 2000.

Iserson, Kenneth. *Demon Doctors: Physicians as Serial Killers.* Tucson, Ariz.: Galen Press, 2002.

Kelleher, Michael, and C.L. Kelleher. *Murder Most Rare.* Westport, Conn.: Praeger, 1998.

Lane, Brian. *The Encyclopedia of Women Killers.* London: Headline, 1994.

Lester, David. *Serial Killers.* Philadelphia: Charles Press, 1995.

Rumbelow, Donald. *The Complete Jack the Ripper.* London: Penguin, 1975.

Schechter, Harold, and David Everitt. *The A to Z Encyclopedia of Serial Killers.* New York: Pocket Books, 1996.

Segrave, Kerry. *Women Serial and Mass Murderers.* Jefferson, N.C.: McFarland, 1992.

Wilson, Colin, and Donald Seaman. *The Serial Killers.* London: True Crime, 1990.

Further Resources

Books

Egger, Steven. *The Killers Among Us*. 2d edition. Upper Saddle River, N.J.: Prentice Hall, 2002.

Newton, Michael. *The Encyclopedia of Serial Killers*. 2d edition. New York: Facts on File, 2006.

Schechter, Harold. *The Serial Killer File*. New York: Ballantine Books, 2003.

Web Sites

Crime Library
http://www.crimelibrary.com

Internet Crime Archives
http://www.mayhem.net/Crime/serial.html

Serial Killers
http://karisable.com/crserial.htm

World Wide Serial Killer Homepage
http://hosted.ray.easynet.co.uk/serial_killers

Index

Page numbers in *italics* indicate images.

About the Author

A former public school teacher (grades 6–8, 1979–86), Michael Newton has published 202 books since 1977, with 18 more scheduled for release from various houses through 2010. His first nonfiction book—*Monsters, Mysteries and Man* (Addison-Wesley, 1979)—was a volume for young readers on cryptozoology and UFOs. His recent reference works include *The Encyclopedia of Serial Killers* (2d edition, 2006) and seven other books from Facts on File (2000–2007), plus the *FBI Encyclopedia* and an *Encyclopedia of Cryptozoology* (McFarland, 2004 and 2005). His history of the Florida Ku Klux Klan, *The Invisible Empire* (University Press of Florida, 2001), won the Florida Historical Society's 2002 Rembert Patrick Award for Best Book on Florida History. A full list of Newton's published and forthcoming titles may be found on his Web site at http://www.michaelnewton.homestead.com.

About the Consulting Editor

John L. French is a 31-year veteran of the Baltimore City Police Crime Laboratory. He is currently a crime laboratory supervisor. His responsibilities include responding to crime scenes, overseeing the preservation and collection of evidence, and training crime scene technicians. He has been actively involved in writing the operating procedures and technical manual for his unit and has conducted training in numerous areas of crime scene investigation. In addition to his crime scene work, Mr. French is also a published author, specializing in crime fiction. His short stories have appeared in *Alfred Hitchcock's Mystery Magazine* and numerous anthologies.